NUFFIELD ECONOMICS & BUSINESS

CW00546419

Teacher's Resources

LONGMAN

Copyright acknowledgements

The Nuffield Economics and Business Project team and the Publishers are grateful for the use of Screen shots on page 131 which are © 1987–1993 Microsoft Corporation. All rights reserved. Reprinted with permission from Microsoft Corporation.

Wherever references to Microsoft® Excel for Windows™ appears in the Teacher's Resources, Microsoft, Excel, and Windows are either registered trademarks and/or trademarks of Microsoft Corporation in the US and/or other countries.

Cover photograph: Paul Brierley

Longman Group Limited
Longman House, Burnt Mill,
Harlow, Essex, CM20 2JE, England
and Associated Companies throughout
the world.

© The Nuffield Foundation 1995

All rights reserved. No part of this
publication may be reproduced, stored
in a retrieval system, or transmitted in
any form or by any means, electronic,
mechanical, photocopying, recording,
or otherwise without the prior written
permission of the Publishers or a
licence permitting restricted copying
issued by the Copyright Licensing
Agency Ltd, 90 Tottenham Court
Road, London, W1P 9HE.

ISBN 0 582 24585 0

First published 1995

Designed and typeset by
Ken Vail Graphic Design, Cambridge

Printed in Singapore by Longman
Singapore Publishers Pte Ltd

The Publisher's policy is to use paper
manufactured from sustainable forests.

Contents

Part 2 The option books

About this book

This book is one of a range of publications which support the Nuffield Economics and Business courses. It provides activities and investigations specifically designed to fit the course requirements, together with notes on their possible uses.

The Nuffield courses are built upon the principle of learning about concepts in context. It is our view that concepts emerge clearly when the situations to which they are relevant are explored. Therefore the activities which make up the student experience are of crucial importance. They provide the context within which the concepts will be made clear. The *Student's Book* is a resource for reference, designed to ensure that the student has access to an adequate knowledge base. The activities are the venue for the learning experience itself.

Some of the activities and investigations described in this book have an accompanying copymaster. These are published separately under the title *Activity Copymasters*. Those activities which do not have copymasters can be adapted by teachers to suit their own circumstances. All the activities and investigations are given a coded number, e.g. 3/2/1. The first number refers to the *stage* of the course for which the activity was designed. The second number refers to the *unit*, and the third to the *activity* itself. This numbering system integrates and identifies all the activities whether or not they include a copymaster. Where a copymaster is available, the symbol **AC** appears in both the text and the guide, which appears on pp. xii–xv.

The contents list gives details of all the activities and investigations referred to in Part 1 of this book. They are not all framed at the same level of difficulty. Some can be adapted to meet a variety of needs. Others need to be selected with thought as to the objective. The activities and investigations guide on pp. xii–xv may help in deciding how they may best be used. This tells you the subject area involved and each activity is coded according to difficulty – I for introductory, S for standard, and C for challenging activities.

The activities are designed to engage, to inform and, sometimes, to excite. They use a range of formats; while many are relatively straightforward case studies, others involve primary investigation, debate, role play, problem solving and decision making, and games. There are far more activities here than teachers can possibly use in the time available. It is intended that a selection should be made, allowing teachers to use only what suits their needs.

Teachers should not feel themselves to be in any way limited to the activities here. They should use whatever materials best fit their needs at the time. However, we hope that these activities will prove to be useful exemplars and demonstrate the range of possibilities.

In the long run, it is to be hoped that teachers will build up a library of resources which will be readily available in the classroom. These should provide considerable raw material for student investigation; indeed, students themselves can contribute much of the material. Perhaps the most important thing is to ensure that suitable storage space is available, which can be easily accessed by the students in the course of their investigations.

Student's Book

Part 1 of this book also acts as a teacher's companion to the *Student's Book*. It provides notes on some of the features of the book and, in particular, gives guidance on the ways in which the working questions may be used. It also makes suggestions about the use to be made of the 'Open Questions'. It identifies some useful sources of information, where necessary including addresses and telephone numbers.

Working questions in the *Student's Book* can, in general, be used in a range of ways. They can be a basis for class discussion or for the student's preparation before the lesson. They can be used to ensure that the student reads in an active and engaged way, or as a basis for homework. Some working questions are an important source of practice in the more numerate sections of the course.

Integration, progression and investigation

These are the three ideas which embody the ethos of the course and form the basis for the course construction. The two subjects are treated in an integrated way, so that no unit is exclusively economics or business studies. The key concepts are explained in ways which show the links between them, integrating the ideas through the problems they help to illuminate. This works not just between the two subjects but also between the four stages of the course.

Progression implies that the early units of the course are built around a gentle incline of difficulty from GCSE. There is a 'ramp', so that, at first, there is great emphasis on an accessible approach. The challenges are then introduced by degrees so that in Stage 2 there is a clear impression of increasing range and difficulty. As the course proceeds there is an expectation that students will bring their prior knowledge to bear on the issues being examined. Thus, revision is a continuous process.

Investigation is the means by which students will make the key concepts of the course familiar and a part of their thought processes. Both primary and secondary research are important and neither should be allowed to expand to exclude the other.

Opening the windows

Progression means that many key concepts are introduced by degrees. Thus, in many places the *Student's Book* just opens a window on a key concept, leaving it to be developed in a subsequent unit. This allows the student to keep an integrated view of the subject matter from start to finish. By the time Stage 4 is reached much of what has gone before is being reviewed and less new material is included. The emphasis is upon consolidation.

IT and data

Throughout this book reference is made to the possibilities for the use of IT. Most such references are accompanied by the symbol **IT**. Many IT references involve the Nuffield Investigations and Data disk. This has been produced in collaboration with the Nuffield Project by the Staffordshire Teachers Group which works with Steve Hurd at the Staffordshire University. Together with accompanying student materials, it is available from Statistics for Education, 5 Bridge Street, Bishop's Stortford, Herts CM23 2JU.

Where a more extensive database is needed, reference is made to *Eureco 94* and *World Trends*. These give data on EU countries and also the USA and Japan, and global data, respectively. Occasionally reference is made to the Regional Trends and UK District Statistics databases. All of these are available from Statistics for Education at the above address, and the price is £35 for each disk, including the Nuffield disk.

These databases run on PC-compatible computers and can be accessed via SECOS. This is a data-handling package which has functions allowing the calculation of growth rates, index numbers and trends. The results can be graphed or mapped. Tables can be annexed and displayed with time lags taken into account. SECOS has been developed by Statistics for Education and is available from it at £50 for the single user version or £150 for a site licence covering networks. This data-handling package is also of interest to geographers and other subject specialists and may already be available generally in your school or college.

Alternatively, there is a utility on the data disks which enables you to export the data in formats which allow access via Excel or Lotus 1-2-3.

The *Data Book* provides an alternative hard copy source of data. It will help students to explore themes which are central to the course. It will inevitably be less extensive than the IT databases taken together, but it will be available for use at home or when other sources of data are not available.

IT and spreadsheets

It is recommended that students use spreadsheets to process and present information wherever this is likely to enhance the learning experience. In the materials for Unit S1/2, 'How is a profit made?' there are spreadsheet exercises which should be accessible to students with no prior experience of spreadsheet use. Subsequent activities gradually assume more and more experience. Later activities simply say that spreadsheets can be used.

All the spreadsheet exercises are worded for use with Excel on a PC-compatible computer. We recommend that, if you are able, you should get this combination of hard and software. (The exercises can be adapted for use with Lotus.) For those who need to become familiar with the use of Excel, the Appendix, 'Using Excel', on pp. 130–43 of this book, provides a detailed guide, together with a simple exercise and answers.

To increase accessibility, some of the activities have the spreadsheet formulae included in the book, and early on some answers have been included too. For the most part the answers are in the *Answer Book*.

The portfolio

The portfolio is envisaged as engendering a strong sense of student ownership. It should be based upon investigations in which students themselves have a strong interest.

In many places certain activities are identified as offering scope for portfolio items to be developed. However the possibilities are not limited to those identified. Students should be encouraged to devise their own portfolio investigations and, in particular, local possibilities should be exploited. The portfolio should contain a wide range of material, including the fruits of primary and secondary research.

The case studies

In both the activities and the *Student's Book*, there are many case studies. All of these are based on research done by the Project team. The majority of them are presented as fact and are accurate and real in every sense. Where the case studies have a fictional air about them, they have always been based on knowledge of a real company. When we want to make critical comments we fictionalise the story and disguise the identity of the company. The case studies based on the lives of individuals are almost all genuine cases, as are those based on interviews and including quotes.

The EC and the EU

The change in the name of the EC (European Community) came as we were writing the materials for the project. The policy adopted is to use EC where the reference is to pre-1994 events, and EU (European Union) where the reference is to January 1994 onwards.

The option books

Each of the six options has a separate guide explaining the thinking that underlies the structure of the option books. There are no copymasters for the options but each guide contains 'Pathways for enquiry', ideas which will be useful in pursuing the enquiries of which the options are made up. A fuller introduction to the options is given at the beginning of Part 2 of this book.

The network

Teachers who are introducing Nuffield courses will benefit from being a part of the Nuffield Network. This will provide information on INSET and on additional resources as they become available, and will create a framework for collaboration between teachers in neighbouring areas. If you are not sure how to get involved in this, telephone the Nuffield Curriculum Projects Office to find out. The number is 0171-436 4512.

Good luck!

The Project team hopes you will enjoy teaching the course, and welcomes your comments on and reactions to the resources available.

Activities and investigations

Activity copymaster	Code	Type	Syllabus area/ approach	Grade
AC	1/1/1	Activity	Personal experience	I
AC	1/1/2	Activity	Defining work	I
	1/1/3	Activity	Necessities/luxuries	I
	1/1/4	Activity	Factors of production	I
	1/1/5	Investigation	Job descriptions	S
AC	1/1/6	Hypothesis test	Motivation	S
AC	1/1/7	Activity	Theory X and Theory Y	S
AC	1/1/8	Case study	Motivation	S
	1/1/9	Investigation	Pay	S
AC	1/1/10	Case study	Opportunity cost, added value	S
AC	1/1/11	Activity/debate	Unemployment	S
	1/1/12	Survey	Employment	S
	1/2/1	Investigation	Profit	I
AC	1/2/2	Activity	Profit	I
	1/2/3	Activity	Value added	S
AC	1/2/4	Activity	Supply and demand	S/C
AC	1/2/5	Spreadsheet exercise	Breakeven	S
AC	1/2/6	Spreadsheet exercise	Profit and loss	S/C
AC	1/2/7	Activity	Business performance	S
	1/2/8	Investigation	Marketing mix	S
AC	1/2/9	Case study	Ethical issues	S
AC	1/2/10	Hypothesis test/ debate	Decision taking	S
AC	1/3/1	Data response	Public expenditure	I
AC	1/3/2	Activity	Values and objectivity	S
AC	1/3/3	Case study	Public expenditure	S
	1/3/4	Investigation	Privatisation	S
	1/3/5	Debate	Privatisation	S
AC	1/3/6	Activity	Privatisation and efficiency	C
	1/3/7	Investigation	Government and business	S
AC	1/3/8	Case study	Private/public sector	S
AC	1/3/9	Activity	History of central planning	S

Activity copymaster	Code	Type	Syllabus area/ approach	Grade
	1/3/10	Investigation	Pricing policy	S
AC	1/3/11	Case study	Market systems	C
AC	2/1/1	Data response	Productivity comparisons	I
AC	2/1/2	Case study	Factor intensity	I
AC	2/1/3	Spreadsheet exercise	Direct and indirect costs	S
AC	2/1/4	Activity	Ratio analysis	I
	2/1/5	Case study	Balance sheets	S/C
	2/1/6	Investigation	Local business	S
AC	2/1/7	Case study	Basic business concepts	I
AC	2/1/8	Spreadsheet exercise	Costs	C
	2/1/9	Investigation	Structural change	S
	2/2/1	Investigation	Local business	S
AC	2/2/2	Activity	Cashflow forecast	C
AC	2/2/3	Data response	Stock management	S
AC	2/2/4	Case study	Human resource management	S
AC	2/2/5	Case study	Centralisation	S
	2/2/6	Activity	Leadership	I
AC	2/2/7	Activity	Leadership	C
AC	2/2/8	Data response	Employee participation	S
AC	2/2/9	Case study	Resource reallocation	S
	2/2/10	Game	Stock market	S
	2/3/1	Activity	Supply and demand	I
AC	2/3/2	Activity	Elasticities	S
	2/3/3	Investigation	Price elasticity	S
AC	2/3/4	Activity	Elasticity and revenue	I
	2/3/5	Activity	Price theory	I
AC	2/3/6	Activity	Competition and monopoly	S
	2/3/7	Investigation	Oligopoly	S
AC	2/3/8	Activity	Oligopoly	S
	2/3/9	Game	Oligopoly	S
	2/3/10	Activity	Prisoner's dilemma	S
	2/3/11	Investigation	Competition	S
	2/3/12	Investigation	Price discrimination	S
AC	2/3/13	Activity	Promotion	S
AC	2/3/14	Problem solving	Congestion	C

Activity copymaster	Code	Type	Syllabus area/ approach	Grade
	3/1/1	Investigation	Business expansion	S
	3/1/2	Investigation	Financial analysis	S
AC	3/1/3	Investigation	Surveys	C
	3/1/4	Activity	Market orientation	I
	3/1/5	Investigation	Gaps in the market	I
AC	3/1/6	Case study	Marketing	S
AC	3/1/7	Yorkie	Marketing	S/C
	3/1/8	Activity	MMC	S
AC	3/1/9	Case study	Market orientation	S
	3/2/1	Brainstorm	Growth	I
AC	3/2/2	Activity	PPP and growth	I
	3/2/3	Investigation	Growth comparisons	I
	3/2/4	Investigation	Growth	S
AC	3/2/5	Activity	Technology and growth	I
AC	3/2/6	Case study	Constraints on growth	S
AC	3/2/7	Activity	Index numbers	S
AC	3/2/8	Activity	External costs	S
	3/2/9	Activity	Environmental accounts	S
AC	3/2/10	Case study	Costs of growth	S
	3/2/11	Investigation	Standard of living	S
	3/2/12	Investigation	Current trends UK	S
	3/2/13	Debate	Role of government	S
	3/2/14	Group work	UK growth	S
AC	3/2/15	Activity	Investment and growth	S
AC	3/3/1	Investigation	UK exports	S
	3/3/2	Investigation	UK imports	I
	3/3/3	Activity	Supply and demand	I
AC	3/3/4	Data response	EC/UK	S
	3/3/5	Hypothesis test	Exchange rates	C
AC	3/3/6	Activity	Exchange rates and prices	S
	3/3/7	Activity	Gains from trade	S
AC	3/3/8	Case study	Competitiveness	S
	3/3/9	Debate	Import controls	S
AC	3/3/10	Activity	GATT	C
AC	3/3/11	Activity	Trade issues	S
	4/1/1	Investigation	Recession	I
AC	4/1/2	Case study	Growth and recession	S

Activity copymaster	Code	Type	Syllabus area/ approach	Grade
	4/1/3	Investigation	Phases of business cycle	S
	4/1/4	Activity	UK trends	S
AC	4/1/5	Data response	Trends and moving averages	S
AC	4/1/6	Data response	Business cycle	S
AC	4/1/7	Data response	Economic performance	S
AC	4/1/8	Activity	Fiscal policy	S
AC	4/1/9	Data response	Change in aggregate demand	S
AC	4/2/1	Investigation	Economies in transition	I
AC	4/2/2	Case study	Adapting to change	S
AC	4/2/3	Mission statement	Corporate culture	S
	4/2/4	Visit	Assisted areas	S
AC	4/2/5	Decision taking	Grant application	C
AC	4/2/6	Discussion	Regional policy	I
AC	4/2/7	Activity	Strategies for change	C
AC	4/3/1	Activity	Career planning	I
	4/3/2	Activity	Personal missions	I
AC	4/3/3	Case study	Business planning	S
	4/3/4	Investigation	Business planning	S
AC	4/3/5	A business plan	Business success/failure	C
AC	4/3/6	Case study	Public sector planning	S
	4/3/7	Activity	Economic forecasts	C
AC	4/3/8	Activity	Economic forecasts	S
AC	4/3/9	Reading	Market systems	S
AC	4/3/10	Reading	Adapting to change	S

Acknowledgements

The development of the courses and resources of the Nuffield Economics and Business Project has been undertaken primarily by the Project Co-directors, Stephen Barnes, David Lines, Jenny Wales and Nancy Wall. This book was written by Stephen Barnes, Jenny Wales and Nancy Wall, with extensive contributions from Alain Anderton (Codsall School, Stafford), Keith Brumfit (Brighton University), David Lines and Steve Reeve (Brighton University).

The seconded teachers who met with the Project team on a fortnightly basis gave unstinting help with the construction of the activities. These were Ian Marcousé (John Ruskin College, Croydon), Nicholas O'Flynn (Beacon Community College, East Sussex), Peter Clarke (Godalming College, Surrey), John Dymott (Farnham College, Surrey), Lynda McKenzie (Richard Hale School, Hertford), Ian Groves (William Ellis School, Camden), Sarah Linklett (Parliament Hill School, Camden) and Barry Martin (Liverpool College). The first four themselves wrote a number of activities.

The IT element in the course owes much to the work of Steve Hurd and the Staffordshire team of teachers who have developed the Nuffield Investigations and Data disk. This has been a most fruitful collaboration.

The spreadsheet exercises were contributed by Jill Turner. The Excel guide, 'Using Excel' (Appendix), was written by Anne Gawlick (both at Godalming College).

The help and support of our administrator, Linda Westgarth, whose contributions were so many and so great that they cannot be briefly described, were essential to both the development work and the final preparation of the book for publication. We would also like to thank our respective partners, all of whom have helped in many ways.

NANCY WALL
Editor

Part 1 The stages

Stage 1: Unit 1 Why do people work?

The unit focuses on

- The nature of work
- Factors of production
- Enterprise and adding value
- Opportunity cost
- Motivation
- Unemployment
- The formal and informal economies
- The changing nature of work

Further ideas encountered

- Specialisation
- Productivity
- National income
- Equity

General advice

This unit is clearly of particular importance as it represents the students' opening experience of the Nuffield course. Like other title questions in Stage 1, 'Why do people work?' is deliberately accessible and open-ended. Instead of the traditional introductory analysis of resources in general, the unit makes *people* its focus. This acknowledges the ultimate human purpose of the two subjects of economics and business and also provides a logical starting point for the investigation of the stage theme: objectives.

It is hoped that the unit title will become a spur to asking many subsidiary questions. Indeed, students are being invited to enter a field of enquiry and, from the outset, to ask real questions. Obviously, there will not always be a final answer and much will depend on their own judgement and interpretation of the relevant data. A great deal of useful and interesting material is constantly appearing in the quality press and in periodicals (including many that are not on the main course list). Good students may utilise published case studies and even explore across subject boundaries into history, geography, sociology and psychology.

All students can investigate the unit question in different dimensions of their own lives. Any part-time employment has obvious potential, while discussion among the students and at home is also very valuable. Above all, personal enquiry and observation are vital. The question 'why do people work?' should become the *students' own* and they should understand that Stage 1, Unit 1 is the best time to begin building their portfolio.

1 What is work?

The early work has a serious purpose but it also needs to be enjoyable. This opening section should be used to stimulate as much questioning and debate as possible. It is also a fertile area for starting the portfolio.

The section title is a genuine problem! It illustrates from the outset the important principle that there are often no fixed or final answers to the questions raised by economics and business studies.

Questions 1a obviously have no 'right' answers. They should serve to open up the ambiguity of the question and to encourage preliminary thoughts about the nature of economic activity. It may be interesting to link these questions with Activity 1/1/2.

Questions 1b highlight the distinction between the individual and society. Question 2 could prompt a good discussion.

Open Questions raise some quite complex issues. It might be most effective to make these questions into an agenda and to give specific students responsibility for preparing a point of view in advance, so providing initial student-to-student stimulus. Item 1 is an interesting question with science fiction/thriller-type implications. The students' own dependency on other people working could be revealed. It would be useful if they appreciated the notion of economic activity as a 'life support system' and recognised, for example, how quickly the shelves of a supermarket would empty without complex and continuous business operations.

AC ❶❶❶ Activity: Why work?

This immediately involves students in making a personal response and should be valuable as a record of their ideas at the outset, which can be compared with their equivalent judgement after completing the unit.

Students can be given the sheet as an exercise without any prior teaching requirements. They should give their answers spontaneously and honestly and could be told that the questions for Part 1 will be asked again at the end of the unit.

The activity may provide some useful information about student attitudes and experience. It also invisibly introduces the idea of opportunity cost.

AC ❶❶❷ Activity: Quotations

This activity could make a discussion agenda and prompt some entries in the student's portfolio. Some of the quotations will be thought very apt, while others will be found provocative! However, important issues are raised. Some of the entries are quite sophisticated and may need explanation.

❶❶❸ Activity: Necessity or luxury?

The students should work in groups with a copy of the

local *Yellow Pages*. Each group can be assigned a few letters of the alphabet, excluding Q-X-Y-Z. They should then record the classified titles starting with those letters and rate them using the following scale:

NN	necessity
N	semi-necessity
LL	luxury
L	semi-luxury

Groups can look up and record the meanings of any titles that they do not understand. Obviously, their ratings will depend on personal judgement, but this does not matter. They can test the importance of an activity by considering what the consequences might be of it ceasing to operate.

While some students use *Yellow Pages*, others could be making a list of ten goods or services that they buy in a typical week, e.g. a bus journey. A whole-group list could be compiled. The demands made by these lists on the factors of production can then be considered, with focus on the students' demand for the labour of other people.

Similarly, the task using *Yellow Pages* lends itself to a combined listing, perhaps sparking some interesting and stimulating debate.

2 What creates work?

The issue of wants and needs should provoke some discussion while it also introduces the distinction between positive and normative statements. The basic concepts necessary for understanding a market economy are introduced without diagrams. This is intentional and the theory will be developed more fully in the units to come.

Questions 2a encourage students to make the connection between demand and work but also prompt them to recognise that real wants do not necessarily create effective demand or the corresponding employment. An early reference to the concept of market failure might be useful.

Questions 2b require further thought about wants and needs and stress the positive/ normative distinction.

Questions 2c are intended to challenge the identity of the ubiquitous 'they'. Market forces can easily be confused with the local council or even with the government!

① ① ④ Activity: Factors of production

Students can be given a small range of relatively simple goods and services and asked to identify the likely inputs necessary for their production. The following are suggested examples:

➤ Cakes   ➤ Petrol
➤ Bed and breakfast ➤ T-shirts
➤ Candles   ➤ Milk

The inputs can then be classified as factors of production. The level of detail is discretionary. It is worth exploring the meaning and role of enterprise. This can be linked with the concept of profit as:
➤ part of the definition for added value
➤ an incentive and reward for risk-taking
➤ a guidance system for all the factors of production.

3 Specialisation and employment

This section highlights the interrelatedness of specialisation, exchange and formal employment. A historical angle is included to reveal the very recent origin of the modern economy and the extraordinary success of specialisation in generating wealth.

Questions 3a arise from Adam Smith's famous description of pin-making. This classic extract will never lose its enormous importance. It is essential that students recognise the immense power of the concept and the dependence of Western society on its applications. Equally, the more problematic implications for the experience of work should emerge. It is interesting to consider the partial reversal of specialisation principles in modern notions of job enrichment, team work and empowerment.

Figure 1 and Questions 3b draw attention to evidence of economic growth during and after the Industrial Revolution. The concept of conversion to current prices may need some introduction.

① ① ⑤ Activity: Job investigations

Students may need guidance regarding their choice of job and firm. Some preparatory work could take place early in the unit. Some liaison with the careers office may be useful. Time constraints may make it necessary to choose between Tasks 3 and 4. This is an item which teachers will probably want to adapt to local circumstances.

The aim of this activity is to discover what jobs require of people and what people require of jobs. It is also necessary to evaluate the extent to which these requirements are met.

Suggested stages

1 Choose a basic career title for which you know that jobs of the type concerned exist in your area. The careers office at school/college or in town is likely to be a useful start. Avoid jobs that are very obscure or unusual. The following offer some suggestions:

➤ Accountant   ➤ Secretary
➤ Farm worker   ➤ HGV driver
➤ Electrician   ➤ Hairdresser
➤ Hotel receptionist ➤ Journalist
➤ Solicitor   ➤ Chef/cook/catering
➤ Welder   assistant
➤ Social worker   ➤ Draughtsman/
➤ Pharmacist   draughtswoman

It would be wise to check first the readiness of a related firm to help you with Tasks 3 and 4.

2 Obtain detailed information about the job concerned. Sources for research might include the careers office, the public library, relevant professional and training bodies or firms and approaching organisations direct. Use this information to produce a job specification for the area of employment concerned.

3 Identify a local firm which employs people in this particular job. Contact the personnel manager or human resources manager to request a short interview, at which time you should ask for any person/job specification in use by the firm and a specific example of a job description for a corresponding post within the firm. (If no formal person/job specification exists, then collect the same information on an informal basis.) Find out why a person is employed to carry out these duties. In what way does this person add value to the firm's product?

4 Arrange an interview with a person holding the job concerned. Try to:

   a)   find out how far they fit the specification for the job

   b)   discover to what extent their experience of the job corresponds with the job description

   c)   assess their motives for taking the job

   d)   evaluate the extent to which the job has fulfilled their needs and expectations.

4 Work and wealth

This is a demanding section, which links the idea of the working population to the specific creation of wealth. This would be a good time to check basic numeracy and to introduce simple data-handling methods.

Questions 4a are based on data that reveal quite well the key changes of the 1980s. Question 2 provides an entry to the important question of productivity.

Questions 4b relate to the first numerate business example. In effect, the students will need to draw up

a very simple profit and loss account. It is important that they understand this calculation properly as it is the basis of so much that follows. The question of profit and loss will be covered fully in Unit 1/2.

Questions 4c focus on sectoral change. The significance of '1990 prices' needs stressing. Some key issues worth exploring include:

➤ the UK's small proportion of employment (and output) accounted for by agriculture

➤ the rather special behaviour of the data for energy and water, due to North Sea oil production, world oil prices and the decline of the coal industry

➤ the recovery of manufacturing output yet the decline in employment; also the underlying decline in the proportional contribution of manufacturing to total output

➤ the significance of 1981 being the trough year in a major recession – and of 1990 being a year of economic downswing

➤ the rise in importance of services of most kinds (and financial services in particular).

The growth of the tertiary sector might tentatively initiate consideration of income elasticity and the post-industrial economy. In addition, students might start to consider how far *does* manufacturing matter?

Questions 4d introduce circular flow problems but still at the simple level of assuming that all income is spent in a single-sector, closed economy. Again, development comes later.

5 The need to work

The examination of Taylor and Taylorism can be seen as one way to answer the question 'Why do people work?' Scientific management remains an important concept but is inadequate as a philosophy of human organisation. (Parallels with other social sciences are interesting to consider?) Mayo and the early human relations school are introduced very briefly. Maslow and McGregor are considered more fully as they offer alternative explanations of 'why people work'.

Questions 5a demand some thought about human relations and motivation. Taylor's ideas often seem unduly reasonable to the students who may be simplistic about motivation and rather influenced by their experience of Saturday jobs! The nineteenth-century background to Taylor's work is important and some comment on industrialisation and the rise of the scientific method may be useful.

Questions 5b start with the theory and move to its application. Finding flaws in Maslow's 'triangle' is important – it is quite a behaviouristic interpretation of human needs. Students may still think some of its implications idealistic: this point is worth discussing.

Questions 5c look at McGregor's celebrated Theories X and Y. Some discussion here is very worthwhile (see Activity 1/1/7 below). Students often feel inclined to accept Theory X – which raises intriguing questions.

AC ❶ ❶ ❻ Investigation: Maslow's Triangle

Testing Maslow's Triangle should enable the students both to see the merits of the theory and to formulate authentic criticism. The students can design their own questionnaire – the more interviewees the better. Evaluation of the results is important. The criticisms of the 'triangle' could be considered in a class discussion.

Before starting the investigation it might be worth challenging the students to produce their own model of needs at work. They often attribute an excessive degree of importance to money. Brainstorming on 'other needs' should produce a wide menu of alternative motivators which might be grouped according to Maslow's hierarchy.

AC ❶ ❶ ❼ Activity: X or Y?

A debate between Theory X and Theory Y students can be interesting. It tends to reveal how attitudes are clustered around underlying value systems. An authoritarian/democratic, conservative/liberal – even pessimistic/optimistic split might emerge.

Before attempting to discuss this concept in a business context, it can be very effective for students to assess their experience of schools and/or (among themselves) senior members of staff in terms of McGregor's theory. This is also a good opportunity to overcome the simplistic tendency to equate Theory Y with 'soft' management and Theory X with 'hard' management. The resulting discussion should be helpful and enable students to think more deeply about the sources of authority and leadership.

AC ❶ ❶ ❽ Activity: The warehouse

This is an intentionally simple case which illustrates the motivational issues explored so far. The students could read the case at home and then work on their decisions – perhaps in pairs – during class time. The actual outcome is given below and might be used to prompt further discussion.

Jane Hillier decided from the outset that Mr Pincombe must either accept early retirement or be transferred to a post in the main office. A new Warehouse Manager would be appointed who was capable of providing positive leadership and entirely reorganising the system of work. All orders and communications with customers would be channelled through the Sales Office. Warehouse staff would form two teams, one serving wholesalers and the other supplying large retailers direct. These teams would work co-operatively, with regular rotation of tasks and clear customer service targets to be met. These targets would be negotiated with the staff concerned. Opportunities for overtime would be made available when necessary.

Bob Tilney gave these plans his full support. Mr Pincombe retired and, three months later, the backlog of orders had vanished while the productivity of the warehouse had improved immensely. Less welcome and more surprising was the cumulative resignation of nearly half the warehouse staff, despite the popularity of the new manager.

6 Rewarding work

This section examines factor rewards to labour and visits the controversial territory of equity. The combination of economics and business perspectives is particularly useful. Students should be able to recognise the realities of labour markets and, again, use demand and supply logic without diagrams. Marginal revenue product theory is implicit but not made formal. The equity debate is likely to be emotive but reference can be made back to market forces as a challenge to the students' thinking. Obviously, they will form their own opinions but they should also be aware of the corresponding business, economic and political implications.

Questions 6a encourage some basic thinking about rewards and their nature. Local examples could be substituted for the cuttings provided. Some small research activity could easily be devised using a local and a national paper.

Questions 6b prompt thought about rates of pay for part-timers, but the real issue is the action of market forces.

Questions 6c address the factors influencing demand and supply in the labour market. The issue of very high salaries makes a good focus for discussion. Students who oppose such rates should consider the alternatives (marginal tax rate question?) and their likely effects. The data in the Distribution of Earnings table puts high salaries in a useful perspective. *Social Trends* has a range of interesting material.

Open Questions take the debate further and might be an opportunity to highlight the importance of trade unions. A whole class discussion or debate is a possibility.

❶❶❾ Activity: Pay and equity

The students should:

a) Choose two well-known occupations and research the current rates of pay and rewards.

b) Test these against each of the factors in the *Student's Book*, page 25.

c) Assess how far these factors explain the rates of pay and try to account for any contradictions.

d) Consider how far these rates of pay are equitable.

It may be desirable to allocate students some occupations to explore. Work on **b)** and **c)** could be made more effective with some careers literature – perhaps using that obtained in Activity 1/1/5. Part **d)** could be assisted by using some material on job evaluation, e.g. Ch. 43 in *Management: Theory and Practice* by Gerald Cole (DP Publications Ltd, 1983).

7 The question of employment

The purpose of this section is to explore the whole issue of employment and unemployment. The concept of opportunity cost is deceptively simple. Students can feel that they have grasped it in a few moments and then fail to recognise that its implications enter every decision-making situation. Figure 11 is quite difficult and may need clarification. Some historical background to the problem of unemployment would be particularly helpful. There are many graphic accounts of the social and psychological reality: *The Road to Wigan Pier* by George Orwell (Penguin), first published in 1937, remains a classic portrayal. The 'work without pay' theme is useful in getting beyond the picture presented by official statistics.

Questions 7a ask students to relate the concept of opportunity cost to the world around and to their own lives. The students should be able to generate some entertaining examples! Their recent choice of A Level subjects might well illustrate the issue quite neatly.

Questions 7b explore the data and introduce the cyclical factor in explaining unemployment.

Open Questions open doors to larger issues and also broaden the debate.

AC ❶ ❶ ❿ Activity: Monique

This activity combines opportunity cost, added value and enterprise in one situation, encouraging students to identify the links between them which are visible in the real world.

AC ❶ ❶ ⓫ Activity: Without work

This is based on the article entitled 'Despair on the breadline' by Heather Mills in the *Independent* of 24 February 1993. It is a very powerful piece of social journalism and, if available, may be worth giving to the students in its original form. There are, of course, many other articles of this type to be found. Once again, there is rich potential for a discussion/debate.

8 Work in the future

The final section is more sophisticated. When does employment represent security (consider 'safe' jobs)? Is life-long employment in decline? Why? Can a job be a trap? Do the students have any examples? Are self-employed people more 'free' and flexible? What about 'portfolio' working? (cf *The Future of Work* by Charles Handy [Blackwell, 1984], or *The Age of Unreason* by Charles Handy [Business Books, 1989] – both extremely stimulating.)

Questions 8a raise some initial questions. The case study family are rather a modern stereotype but do reflect recent social change in some sections of society. The Flynn family could be treated as a discrete exercise or could prompt discussion and private thought. The question of education and training raises serious issues of contemporary interest and can be related to the changing objectives of personnel management. Sex roles always arouse strong feelings among the students and the

experience of Sarah Flynn will now seem more typical for women. Self-employment is a possible goal for some students? The issue of formal/informal work and work/leisure relate back to issues raised earlier in the unit. A reconsideration of Maslow prompts the question of self-actualisation as a driving force in motivation by higher order needs.

Questions 8b focus on the 'boundary breaking' theme. Students might consider how far these boundaries have been broken to date and how far the trend is likely to go?

Open Questions are a full agenda for debate. If time permits, an open discussion of these issues would be a good way to conclude the unit.

❶ ❶ ⓬ Activity: Employment Survey

Instructions to students:
Make a brief survey – among at least 20 students – to find out the proportion of parents/guardians with
➤ full-time permanent jobs
➤ part-time jobs
➤ self-employment
➤ no employment.

a) Break down your results by the sex of parents. What are your main findings?
b) How far is your sample likely to be typical of the UK population at large? Try to offer an explanation to account for the significant ways in which you think your sample varies from the national norm.

Relevant data can be found in *Social Trends* (CSO) and the *Employment Gazette* (Department of Employment).

This could be a class or school/college-wide activity. Results could be shown on pie charts. The supplementary questions will require some student awareness of the characteristics of the class/ school/college population.

Stage 1: Unit 2 How is a profit made?

The unit focuses on

- Profit
- The motives for running a business
- Demand, supply and equilibrium price
- Market research
- Market segmentation
- Break-even analysis
- Profit and loss accounts
- Market share
- The marketing mix

Further ideas encountered

- Corporate culture
- Niche markets
- Cash flow
- Decision making and risk
- Business ethics

General advice

This unit develops the idea of profit as both an accounting identity and a dynamic reward for economic activity. The concept of added value is then used to show how combining the factors of production can generate a surplus under competitive conditions. This is then related to the human objectives of operating a business enterprise.

The consideration of demand, supply and price is elementary and should be approached in a strongly applied context. The principles of market forces then lead directly to the process of market research. This, in turn, opens discussion of market segments and niches.

The work on profit proceeds through simple breakeven analysis and costing, including the contribution principle. The Profit and Loss Account is explained from first principles and then extended through the typical format used by a large organisation.

The final sections look at market share and the construction of a marketing mix while using the economic concepts already learned. The unit ends with consideration of profit in its wider social and ethical context.

The goal throughout is for students to address academic ideas in a spirit of vigorous enquiry. A series of practical contexts is offered as the best means to ignite this process. Why does an enterprise exist? In what ways is value added? How can a surplus be generated within a competitive market? These are questions that cannot be asked too often and can be directed at any type of economic organisation.

The unit provides a good opportunity to examine both smaller local enterprises and large national or multinational corporations. Small firms have the great advantage of simplicity in their essential operations and organisational structure: the means by which a profit (or loss) is made is relatively transparent. Large firms provide an insight into the wider economy and, for students, can convey the romantic flavour of big business. The local and national news media should be valuable in this unit and students can be encouraged to follow relevant stories and record findings in their portfolio. In this respect, critical perspectives on firms and economic activity are important. The idea that economic and business decisions carry much wider political and moral dimensions is integral to the course.

1 People and firms

This section carries the thread of human needs from Unit 1 into the consideration of profit. Adding value is a key theme which recurs throughout the course.

❶❷❶ Investigation: Why run a business?

The obvious answer is 'to make money'. This investigation provides a chance for students to investigate below the surface of the obvious and perhaps to gain some insight into the real motives of a local entrepreneur. The work on motivation in Stage 1 ought to supply some clues and directions for research.

It may be most appropriate for the students to work in pairs or small groups. They need to find an entrepreneur who is willing to discuss, fairly openly, his/her reasons for running a business. This could take the form of a structured or unstructured interview. Students could produce short, written reports outlining their conclusions and these might form a useful portfolio entry. A final plenary discussion on the topic could also be valuable.

AC ❶❷❷ Activity: Speaking of profit

These quotes provide an opportunity for the students to explore the nature and meaning of profit. Quotes (1) are fairly philosophical, while Quotes (2) are more applied in nature. The material can be used as a written exercise but would be equally suitable as the basis for a class discussion.

❶❷❸ Activity: How is value added?

The idea of this activity is for the students to explore real sources of added value. For a given enterprise they can identify the inputs, the outputs and each process that adds value. It is likely that some assumptions will have to be made and a certain amount of guesswork is perfectly reasonable.

In many manufacturing enterprises the logic of added value is fairly straightforward, although there may be intangible factors that add value at the final sale. In service industries the elements of added value are often less obvious, e.g. service, ambience or reputation. It is important that students think carefully about the activity. For instance, it is easy to appreciate how the processing and canning of haricot beans and tomato sauce adds value. But students can miss the point that a 'Heinz' label adds more value than the name of a supermarket.

The choice of enterprise for this analysis can be based on accessible local enterprises or on national firms of particular interest (a good early opportunity to obtain some annual reports and accounts). Some suggestions are given below:

Local	National
➤ Second-hand car dealer	➤ Sainsbury's
➤ Bakery	➤ Grand Metropolitan
➤ Builder	➤ Prudential
➤ Butcher	➤ British Airways
➤ Cafe	➤ Barclays Bank
➤ Travel agent	➤ British Steel
➤ Hairdresser	➤ BP
➤ A dairy farmer	➤ EMI

Inputs

These should be itemised in as much detail as possible and can follow the basic logic of a detailed profit and loss account. They could then be classified as specific factors of production.

Outputs

The main products or product ranges can be identified. This may be a good opportunity to emphasise the legitimacy of services as 'products' and students can practise the recognition of output from service industry.

Sources of added value

These need careful identification. There is a danger that students will regard the process of adding value as a rather mechanical sequence of formally productive operations. In this respect, they need attention drawn to the numerous intangible sources of added value, e.g. the quality of packaging or the display in a shop window. The enquiries made by the students could usefully focus on the 'package' of benefits that the consumer expects to derive from purchase of the product. These are the springs of value and should help to highlight the contribution of the firm concerned.

The work itself could take the form of a short report, or the students could be given a simple handout to complete. Group presentations to the class are also possible, perhaps illustrated by a sample of the product or some promotional literature?

2 Markets

This is a very important section which lays foundations for later analysis. The more practical the illustrations used to illustrate the principles of demand and supply are, the better.

AC ❶ ❷ ❹ Activity: Market forces in action

This activity is designed to show students how supply and demand analysis can be used. Although they have not yet been introduced to elasticities, they should be able to make qualitative comments indicating some understanding of the variations in response to price changes which may occur. Some of the questions may seem difficult at this stage in the course, but most of them can be answered on a common-sense level and that is acceptable.

Scenario 3 introduces tax incidence. However it is not necessary to belabour the idea at this stage: it is covered fully in Stage 3, in the context of tariffs.

There is a good deal of scope here for class discussion. It would be helpful if the students could see for themselves how analysis can deepen the discussion of the issues. This activity is best approached when students have achieved a reasonable grasp of the concepts.

3 Market research

Students usually enjoy work on this theme. Some practical activity is possible; this is probably more valuable when carried out in the community but research in school/college can still be useful. A local market research or marketing agency may well provide some case examples and (free) back issues of a marketing magazine. The Market Research Society in London welcomes educational enquiries and can supply some good materials.

The pressure of time may make it impossible to undertake practical activity at this point. There is an extensive market research activity with a copymaster, suggested for use with 'How do firms expand?' (S3/1).

4 Targeting the market

This is a basic introduction to the idea of segmentation and follows logically from market research. The simple idea that people are not the same and that their sources of satisfaction in consumption differ can open a preliminary discussion. By what criteria can consumers be divided into groups? Would these criteria be different for supermarkets and newspapers? How should producers respond? The thread then leads towards analysing and understanding clusters of consumer wants and relating these to product ranges and product variants.

There are many products/industries which offer a good entry to the theme. Models/model variants for cars, types of hotel, different chains of boutiques, etc. all work well. Some product brochures and allied advertisements can make the discussion more real.

The students can gain a good deal of pleasure and insight from work on segmentation as it arises so strongly from human feelings, characteristics, lifestyles, etc. The whole subject is dealt with in more depth in 'How do firms expand?' (S3/1) when wider reading will be more appropriate.

5 Profit or loss?

It is very important that students are not discouraged by this first sustained encounter with numerate analysis. Those who are taking other numerate subjects to an advanced level will find no problem with the work here, but many students seem ready to believe that any numerate approach is 'hard'. In reality, the reverse is probably true.

The idea of 'making a profit' is essentially quite appealing to most students. They need to become familiar with the arithmetic and to develop a sense of curiosity about the phenomenon. It would be good to see them becoming adept at making quick profit calculations, at estimating outcomes, at evaluating business propositions – and considering more carefully possible answers to the title of this unit. Positive use of a simple calculator is important. Some students are very reluctant to make impromptu, personally directed enquiries once numerate data are involved. Plenty of informal examples and the use of a database should help.

The media contain much commentary on profitability and some portfolio tracking studies might be launched at this stage. Again, use of company annual reports can be valuable. If there is a co-operative local firm or a family business run by one of the students' relatives, it may be possible to find some authentic data, but many small firms maintain strict confidentiality in this area.

AC ❶ ❷ ❺ Activity: Alison breaks even

IT The objective of this exercise is to reinforce the concept of breakeven by enabling students to see immediately the effect of changing any of the variables.

The copymaster provides the necessary formulae so that even the least confident will be able to produce a table of data from which to see the breakeven output and profit/loss at each level of output. By following these instructions, the data in the table can easily be converted to the familiar breakeven graph, using the spreadsheet to its full potential to illustrate changes in variables.

A completed table and graph is provided in the *Answer Book*.

The assumption is that the contribution is £2, and that full capacity output is 1000. Profit at full capacity is £1000. The breakeven output is 500. If the price is £7, breakeven output is 250, and profit at full capacity is £3,000. If fixed costs rise to £1,500, breakeven output is 750, and profit at full capacity is £500. Alison would cease production if the price were less than £4. If fixed costs are set at the higher figure (£3,000), breakeven output rises to 1,500.

Although the essential arithmetical and graphical skills necessary for breakeven analysis are very simple, many students fail to internalise the concept and make it their own. One solution is for them to gain real familiarity with the logic of breakeven and contribution through plentiful examples and self-directed experiments. Once familiar with the spreadsheet format, they can enter their own data into the basic model and devise and test their own case examples.

The danger of the activity is its 'neatness'. It is obviously important that students recognise the dynamic and unpredictable nature of business reality where breakeven assumptions are only tentative approximations. They should also realise that qualitative variables can be at least as important in the real process of decision making.

In using the spreadsheet, students can start with a series of simple 'what if ...' calculations. They can then divide into pairs/groups and devise cases of their own. These could be word-processed and distributed to other groups for testing. Some more general discussion of outcomes could close the activity.

AC ❶ ❷ ❻ Activity: Bharatya Pictures Ltd

Here the objective is to familiarise students with the component parts of the profit and loss account, using the spreadsheet as a tool for manipulating data.

Working through the questions should enable them to see how increases/decreases in costs and revenues can affect the final profit figure.

IT advice: creating a spreadsheet for a profit and loss account is a straightforward exercise and can be carried out with only limited knowledge of Excel. The formulae to use are as follows:

Bharatya Pictures Ltd
Profit and loss account for the year ended
30 September 1990

	1990	1989
	£	£
Turnover	449226	178388
Cost of Sales	369958	127752
GROSS PROFIT	=B6–B7	=C6–C7
Administrative expenses	24880	32642
OPERATING PROFIT	=B8–B9	=C8–C9
Interest receivable	1526	455
NET PROFIT BEFORE TAX	=B10+B11	=C10+C11
Tax	14635	5533
NET PROFIT AFTER TAX	=B12–B13	=C12–C13
Dividends	32000	
RETAINED PROFIT for the year	=B14–B15	=C14–C15
RETAINED PROFIT brought forward	14242	1326
RETAINED PROFIT carried forward	=B16+B17	=C16+C17

The questions can be worked through using either the capabilities of Excel or pen, paper and calculator. The answers are given in full in the *Answer Book*.

AC ❶ ❷ ❼ Activity: The top ten

In this activity students have the opportunity to become familiar with the largest UK business enterprises and to carry out some related numerate analysis. The information given here is extracted from *The Times 1000 1994* (a useful reference book and available in larger libraries) and can be updated from later editions. This might be a good stage at which to send off for a corresponding set of company annual reports and accounts. These will clarify and extend the data given here as well as providing interesting information on organisational structure, physical operations and product range. They also give a first glimpse of formal published accounts and will be very useful in Stage 2.

The questions aim to highlight the different applications of the term 'profit' and ask students to assess possible

reasons for the proportional differences between firms. This is also time for first thoughts about the relative size and performance of business enterprise. Students need to understand that profit as a surplus is generated by both a stock and a throughput of scarce resources. Here the concept of profit margin is explored but, if desired, the notion of return on capital could also be given a quick introduction (ideally at the students' initiative). It will, in any case, be given a full explanation in 'What is efficiency?' (S2/1).

There is a potential extension to this activity, which could run right through the first term of the course. Working in groups, pairs or as individuals, the students could track news and progress of a company 'adopted' from the list. This might involve sending off for its annual/interim reports, preparing a record of its key statistics and financial performance over a period, monitoring its share price and keeping relevant news cuttings. Such work could also make ideal material for a portfolio feature.

6 Winning market share

This is very much an introduction to the topic and some simple calculations and lively examples are the best starting point. Some thought about the significance of market share would be valuable (economies of scale, stability of business, competitive power, etc.), although this need only be at a very elementary level. Links to what has already been learned should be emphasised as much as possible. For example, the movement of demand curves may represent a gain or loss of market share. Dynamism is important: many texts and examples tend to assume static or single movement models which do not resemble the restlessness of real markets.

IT There are often good articles on market share in the financial press, including analysis of supermarket chains (CD-ROM could be helpful here). The Nuffield Investigations and

Data disk has some comprehensive material on the car and music industries.

7 The marketing mix

Once again, this theme is only presented here at foundation level and is fully developed in Stage 3. Generally there is a danger that the marketing mix becomes a rather descriptive topic with a lack of conceptual structure. In fact, it is an ideal area for the integration of economics and business. The distinction between price and benefits is fundamental. Work on price can build on knowledge of demand and supply theory, while benefits can be related to the market model and the concept of consumer surplus. The link forward to profit should be made explicit.

Detail generally is not very important. The students should get used to assessing the mix at work in plenty of familiar products (services as well as goods) and there is rich scope for portfolio entries.

❶❷❽ Activity/Investigation: Making the mix

An optimum marketing mix has to be designed for every product. As a construction, the mix must be tightly integrated and highly flexible. Conventional textbook coverage often fails to recognise that the elements in the mix vary enormously in their relative importance by firm, by product and over time.

In this activity the students can think through the implications of a flexible and dynamic marketing mix. The requirement is to show how and why the mix ingredients vary from product to product (or firm to firm).

Some possible products for analysis include:
➤ Newspapers
➤ Chocolate bars
➤ Pensions
➤ Bicycles
➤ Farm machinery
➤ Private healthcare
➤ Petrol sales
➤ Hi-fi
➤ Theatre tickets
➤ Dog food

There are two possible approaches.

a) As an investigation, the students (solo/pairs/groups) can conduct primary research into the mix of local firms or branches of national organisations. Excessive detail should be avoided or the whole exercise will become too time-consuming and clogged with descriptive material. It is particularly important to reveal the relative priority given to each mix element, with commentary on the actual or likely reasons. If students have analysed one or two firms each, then a class presentation would allow comparison and relevant discussion.

b) As a classroom-based activity, students can consider a small range of different firms/products. The likely mix of ingredients can then be listed and arranged in a projected order of priority. Reasons can be given and some plenary discussion should be valuable. It must be emphasised that students are only 'sketching' the likely elements and priorities in a credible mix and, clearly, they cannot enter into detail. However, specific examples would be useful and can add life to the activity.

8 Profit in perspective

This last section is designed to raise the human and ethical implications of profit and profit–driven activity. These issues will recur throughout the course and it is essential that students see them as central rather than peripheral. Plenary discussion or role play can be very stimulating but some small group work may be necessary for less confident students to find a voice.

It would be valuable if the idea of externalities was introduced here, even if only in the most informal and simple terms. It would provide an open-ended retrospect on costing and the price mechanism, while broadening the ethical debate to include environmental and social dimensions.

AC ❶ ❷ ❾ Activity: The Co-operative Bank

The copymaster contains an article which discusses the ethical policy of the Co-operative Bank. Students are asked to consider the extent to which the bank's policy reflects an ethical stand, a useful marketing ploy or a combination of the two.

AC ❶ ❷ ❿ Activity: Should farms go organic?

The intention of this activity is to hold a plenary debate about the issue of organic foods and farming. This may be best arranged at the end of the unit period or could be scheduled to open the hypothesis-testing activity on the same subject. The whole topic is one of real contemporary interest and is often quite high on students' own agendas. Within any teaching group there is likely to be a range of opinion from the committed to the cynical or dismissive.

It will be desirable for the debate to be reasonably informed and closely linked to the economic and business ideas raised in the syllabus and explored in the *Student's Book*. There are three suggested approaches.

1 A traditional debate could address a motion such as 'Farms should adopt organic methods of production'.

2 A looser class debate could tackle the same issue, perhaps through a planned agenda which ensures consideration of the arguments for and against and the different interest groups affected.

3 A role play can work well with small groups of students accepting advocacy of different sectional interests. Groups could prepare their position in advance with Copymaster material used as prompts. This may be most effective if each group receives only their appropriate prompts, ensuring an element of surprise in the arguments put forward. The format of a radio or TV debate/discussion could be adopted with the teacher or a student as chairperson.

Stage 1: Unit 3 What should the state provide?

The unit focuses on

- The private and public sectors
- Public expenditure
- Taxation
- Market orientation
- Privatisation
- Regulation
- The legal framework for business
- Central planning
- Mixed economies

Further ideas encountered

- Productivity
- Efficiency
- Competition
- Accountability
- Equity
- Trade-offs
- Opportunity cost

General advice

This unit starts by looking at the role of the government in everyone's life, and how it has grown over time. Then it takes up a number of important issues, ones that have influenced the way we think about the government and its involvement in the economy. We consider the ways in which public and private sector objectives differ and how government affects business. Later, the unit looks at how the search for efficiency has led to big changes in the role of governments all over the world.

Up to this point, the government has figured relatively little in the questions addressed by the course. Thinking about the public sector brings in a new dimension. The unit is predominantly concerned with economic issues which provide a backdrop to the business world.

The questions in the *Student's Book* are quite big ones, many involving value judgements. However, it is not intended that students spend too long on them. At this stage in the course, the objective is to get a feel for the scope of government activity, rather than to produce definitive answers to some very knotty problems. Not all of the questions need to be examined: a suitable selection can be made.

Some of the issues addressed here will date quite quickly and it will be important in the future to supplement the materials provided with detail on newer ones.

1 What do you expect from the government?

While working on this section, the student will be developing important background knowledge. Many major policy issues can be highlighted, opening the student's eyes to the complexity of the organisation of a modern economy. In gradually opening up questions of efficiency and equity, the unit lays foundations for work in subsequent units.

Questions 1a open up the very individual question of what *ought* to be provided. Students can make their own 'shopping list', and then construct arguments in favour of each item. In groups, they can compare notes, develop their arguments and decide how objective they are being. (Activity 1/3/2 points up the distinction between subjective and objective statements.) If the group is able to produce a consensus view, this would be worth attempting.

Figure 1, Government expenditure, offers an opportunity to investigate the government's priorities. It also requires students to distinguish between real growth and inflation.

AC ❶❸❶ Activity: UK public spending

This uses some basic numeracy skills in a new context. The same data are given as in Figure 1 in the *Student's Book*, but with questions designed to reinforce knowledge of percentages. If possible students should update the figures using the *National Income Blue Book*.

AC ❶❸❷ Activity: Whose view is it?

Students will need to practise making the distinction between subjective and objective statements. They can do this in the context of their views about what they want from the government.

They could follow this up by discussing, in groups, the implications of differing values for the decision making process.

It would be possible to adapt this activity using the positive/normative distinction, if that is the preferred approach.

2 The growth of expenditure and taxation

This section aims to develop some historical perspective, as well as to provide basic information on the role of the state.

IT Questions 2a ask students to consider whether there is a link between the size of the public sector and the standard of living. They will need some help in deciding how best to define the standard of living, as well as in finding suitable data. This is a good opportunity for using an IT database such as Eureco. Again, practice with percentages is encouraged, as in Questions 2d.

Students should be encouraged to collect information from newspapers on the Budget, which will be likely to be announced near the time at which they study taxation and government spending.

Much of the detail of the existing tax system is captured in the case study on Mary and Tom Vine's tax bills. Mary's basic salary is just a little above the current average male manual earnings, so her case illustrates the operation of the main taxes in a fairly representative way.

AC ❶❸❸ Activity: Migraine cure gives NHS a headache

The purpose here is deliberately to highlight the open-ended nature of some government expenditure commitments, so that students can see the importance of deciding on priorities with due regard to opportunity costs.

3 A shifting role for government

The opening case study is intended to put the role of government into its political context. It would be appropriate to investigate the views of other political parties if students are interested.

❶❸❹ Investigation: Council house sales

Information on council house sales locally is relatively easy to obtain. The local housing office or councillor may be able to help. If you can network with other schools through TTNS or E-mail, this may help. Questions which can be explored include:

➤ How have council housing policies affected the availability of housing for rent in the area?
➤ What is the incidence of homelessness?
➤ How might the changing pattern of home ownership affect a small building business?

4 Markets, privatisation and regulation

It may be that the privatisation of British Rail (BR) will cease to be an issue within the life of these resources; however, the question of whether railways should be subsidised may not. Regulation will certainly continue to be an open issue.

It would be helpful for students to investigate the effects of market orientation, either in a private sector context or in an area of the public sector which is currently attempting to become more customer-friendly. This will require suitable contacts with someone in each sector who is prepared to talk about it. Students should be aware of the existence of a large area of the economy in which objectives are different from those of both individuals and private sector business. The aim is to explore the differences in objectives, and their implications.

❶❸❺ Activity: Debating privatisation

The class can be divided into groups, each of which prepares one side of the argument, and then debate it. Possible topics include privatisation versus nationalisation in general, or applied to a particular case, e.g. water.

A possible starting point

Consider the water supply industry. Is it a natural monopoly? What special problems does the industry face? What has been the effect of privatising it, on both consumers and producers? What reasons can you give as to why privatising it might not have been a good idea?

One would hope that students would define the problem, i.e. steadily increasing demand, rising with income and a flat rate payment system, not related to consumption, together with rising costs of additional provision.

Find out what kind of regulation controls another privatised natural monopoly. Are the public effectively protected by this regulatory activity?'

An alternative starting point

British Rail was taken into public ownership in the 1940s. As car ownership increased, there was less and less chance that, as a whole, it might make a profit or even just cover its costs, despite frequent fare increases. In particular, some commuter services and many rural branch lines can never be profitable. If they are to run at all, they must be given a government subsidy.

Why might you want these services to be kept going by the government, using a subsidy financed by tax revenue, even though their users' fares cannot cover the costs of the service? Is it essential to keep BR in public ownership if the rail network is to be preserved? Can railways reduce congestion? To what extent are roads subsidised at the expense of railways?

AC ❶❸❻ Activity: The effects of privatisation on efficiency

This activity presents some evidence on the subject and points towards some areas for further investigation.

5 What does business expect from the government?

This is no more than a brief introduction to the relationship between business and the government.

Questions 5a expect the student to consider the effect of some loss of trade union bargaining power in general, rather than to explore the effect of individual measures. Comments such as 'employers will be under less pressure to concede wage increases' would be acceptable.

The stakeholder concept, which will recur throughout the course, is introduced here, and students are asked to apply it in Questions 5b.

❶❸❼ Investigation: How government affects an individual business

Students may either visit and study a local business, or a local manager may be prepared to come in and talk. This may be positive or negative in its effects. If more than one business can be investigated, then comparisons will be possible. Students will need to think through beforehand the questions which need to be asked. Possible issues include the effect of employment legislation, the resources needed to deal with tax and insurance payments, the availability of grants or advice from government bodies, the effect of changes in interest rates.

AC ❶❸❽ Activity: Business and the community

This activity takes a different angle – looking at business provision of public facilities in New York and the way in which business may accept a degree of responsibility for the community in which it is located.

6 What does the European Union provide?

One way to give this topic some immediacy would be to encourage students to collect news items involving the EU, but a period of several weeks would be needed.

An important objective at this point is simply to make students aware of the scope of EU activity. Brainstorming the aspects of the EU which they have come across would be helpful. Identifying the costs and benefits of EU activity to date, e.g. the effect of the CAP on food prices and farm incomes would also be worthwhile. The Consumers' Association has campaigned on this for years, pointing out the high cost of the CAP to consumers. Its address is 2 Marylebone Road, London NW1. There is an article on this issue in the March 1993 edition of *Which?* magazine.

Students should be strongly encouraged to address the open questions at the end of the section, exploring their own attitudes to the EU.

7 All in the public sector: central planning

AC ❶❸❾ Activity: The historical perspective

The copymaster provides a list of events, designed simply to help the students to keep track of the chronological order of things and to enable them to pick up the connections between political events in different countries. It provides additional background with which to tackle some of the questions in the *Student's Book*. It is not confined to the history of planned economies. Students could be encouraged to use this as a basis for expanding their knowledge by writing in additional events as they become aware of them, and by updating the list when appropriate. This is an exercise which could continue for the duration of the course.

8 Making the mixed economy work better

This section takes up a number of issues which have been touched on earlier. The open questions at the end are intended to lead to some degree of overview of the unit. There is much scope here for picking up more recent issues relating to the role of the government.

❶❸❿ Investigation: Pricing policy

Students could investigate any of the following pricing questions, or any other public sector pricing problem in which they are interested:

➤ the level of prescription charges
➤ charges for opticians and/or dental services
➤ BR fares
➤ museum or gallery entrance charges.

Questions to be addressed

Does the price charged deter potential users/consumers? Should the charges be raised/reduced? If charges were raised, to what use might the resulting funds be put?

Possible hypotheses

➤ Fare reductions for rail journeys would increase revenue and reduce congestion.

➤ An increase in prescription charges would raise revenue which could be spent on reducing hospital waiting lists and would entail little loss of welfare.

➤ Alternatively, frame other questions as hypotheses

and see whether they are confirmed by your investigations.

AC ❶ ❸ ⓫ Activity: The internal market in health care

By looking at the practicalities of the internal market, this activity highlights some of the issues which arise when a market system is introduced into a previously non-market organisation. It may be possible to use it as a focus for discussion or debate or, as suggested in the copymaster, to use it as background for a local investigation.

Stage 2: Unit 1 What is efficiency?

The unit focuses on

- Measuring efficiency: return on capital employed, productivity
- Efficiency in business
- Fixed and variable factors
- Diminishing returns
- Economies and diseconomies of scale
- Direct and indirect costs; overheads
- Total, average, fixed, variable and marginal costs
- Contribution; choosing the most profitable output
- Technical and allocative efficiency
- Competition
- Market forces
- Reallocation of resources

Further ideas encountered

- Factor intensity
- Corporate culture and management structures
- Exit and entry, competition, product differentiation
- Motivation
- Normal and supernormal profit

General advice

This unit has to convey a large number of ideas which are either needed later on in the course or are of considerable importance in terms of their place in the subject. The objective is to make all these ideas comprehensible by explaining them in context. Sometimes the context is real, as in the case studies. At other times the examples given are invented in order to give practice in the use of the ideas. Invention is usually necessary when costs are under discussion because it is so hard to get data which are both real and manageable.

There is a tendency for all of the most attractive examples used in teaching these concepts to be drawn from the manufacturing sector. It is all too easy to create the impression that manufacturing is of paramount importance in business. Where possible, there should be a balance of examples drawn from all sectors, giving due weight to the growing importance of services.

Throughout this unit there is a need for students to have some experience of industrial visits to draw upon.

1 Aims, objectives and decisions

This opening section introduces technical and allocative efficiency, and the framework of business decisions.

The opening case study, 'Barton's Boxes', is intended to initiate thinking that will be of relevance to this and to the next unit. The students will quickly recognise that the company is a 'straw man'. They should be encouraged to look beyond the obvious factors such as incompetent leadership and out-of-date, depreciated machinery. This example can draw attention to staff and their morale, communications and culture, working capital management and opportunity cost. A preliminary discussion about the merits of holding stock, either through over-production or on a 'just-in-case' basis would be valuable. The suggested improvements should carry some indication of how they will lead to better use of scarce resources.

This is a chance for students to review the possibilities, albeit in a fairly uninformed way. It introduces the material not just in this unit but the next one also.

Further on in this section students are invited to explore their own experience of decision taking. Most students will probably choose decisions that have arisen in their school/college career to date. However, it would be worth broadening the discussion to include part-time work, holidays, sports opportunities, membership of clubs or societies, etc.

2 Taking production decisions

Various aspects of productivity, factor intensity, production systems and direct and indirect costs are grouped together in this section.

Direct and indirect costs
We will be asking students to learn this and the fixed/variable approach to costs, each being useful in different circumstances. The Solid Plastics example has been created deliberately so that a single scenario can be used for both approaches.

AC ❷❶❶ Activity: Productivity growth rates

An international comparison of productivity growth rates. This requires students to learn something about the interpretation of index numbers. (This will be developed further in Stage 3.) At this stage students will not be able to answer the questions in a very informed way. The objective is to draw their attention to the comparisons. It might be worthwhile to return to these figures after study of 'How do we increase efficiency?' (S2/2)

AC ❷❶❷ Activity: Choosing the best production methods

An important objective here is to get students to think about the relative costs of labour and capital. Ideally, the questions should be extended to draw upon students' investigations of local industries.

AC ❷❶❸ Spreadsheet activity: Solid Plastics

IT This activity uses the data in the *Student's Book* which is included on the copymaster for convenience. It requires students to cover the same

ground as Questions 2e, but using a spreadsheet. It reinforces the distinction between direct and indirect costs, and enables students to make the appropriate calculations on costs, revenue and profit. Students can use the potential of the spreadsheet to see and analyse the effect of changes in output.

The copymaster provides a structure to the spreadsheet but leaves the student to differentiate between direct and indirect costs when inputting data.

The student tasks are self-explanatory. The completed spreadsheet below shows the correct formulae for the spreadsheet; these can be used to advise students as they work on their calculations. The answers are in the *Answer Book*.

Solid Plastics formulae

Solid Plastics Direct and indirect costs

		25% increase
OUTPUT	80 000	=B4*1.25
SELLING PRICE	1.5	1.5
DIRECT COSTS	£	
Wages	36 000	=B8*1.25
Raw mats	10 000	=B9*1.25
Electricity	3000	=B10*1.25
TOTAL DIRECT COSTS	=sum(B8:B10)	=sum(C8:C10)
INDIRECT COSTS (overheads)		
Rent	9000	9000
Rates	1600	1600
Insurance	1500	1500
Electricity	1000	1000
Depreciation	7500	7500
TOTAL INDIRECT COSTS	=sum(B14:B18)	=sum(C14:C18)
TOTAL COSTS	=B11+B19	=C11+C19
TOTAL REVENUE	=B4*B5	=C4*C5
OPERATING PROFIT	=B23−B21	=C23−C21
PROFIT MARGIN%	=B24/B23*100	=C24/C23*100
Average direct costs/unit	=B11/B4	=C11/C4
Average indirect cost/unit	=B19/B4	=C19/C4
Average total cost/unit	=B21/B4	=C21/C4

3 Taking financial decisions

The balance sheet, some simple ratios and the concept of working capital are introduced here as sources of information on which decisions may be based.

Students are introduced straightaway to the vertical format of the balance sheet, with a simple example. They will then need some practice in order to interpret a formal annual report and accounts.

At this point, it would be desirable for students to begin to explore the situation in which the firm is quite inefficient but is nevertheless very profitable because it has some monopoly power. It is to be hoped that students will identify this situation themselves in the course of group discussion and debate.

AC ❷❶❹ Activity: Return on capital employed

This activity is a simple calculation exercise. It should, however, be possible to consider what ROCE does and does not tell us, and also whether the figures in the exercise can be explained, e.g. by BP's problems or by the recession conditions of the time.

AC ❷❶❺ Activity: Picture-a-Frame

This is a practical exercise in the interpretation of a profit and loss account and a balance sheet.

4 Taking marketing decisions

This section aims to build bridges between marketing decisions and the nature of allocative efficiency. Students are encouraged to think about what they observe in the world around them and what the implications are in terms of resource allocation. Marketing is dealt with in much more detail in both Stage 1 and Stage 3; it is included here just so that it can take its place in the general overview of business decisions.

5 Human resource decisions

Issues associated with management structures are introduced here but will be much more fully developed in the next unit.

In the questions after the BP case study, we would hope that students will explore the potential of the reorganisation to allow faster communication and a flexible response to change. Linking this case with what was learned about motivation in Stage 1 creates a chance to revise and integrate related ideas.

❷❶❻ Investigation: A local business

At about this point, it is highly desirable that students should make an industrial visit, which should perform a number of different functions. It could be to any small, but not too small, business producing goods or services or both. It should not be in the retailing sector, which is already fairly familiar to most. If possible, it should look at the functional areas studied already. It should be set up in such a way that division of labour and economies of scale can be observed, or reviewed in retrospect. If students can set up their own visits in groups, so much the better. Each group should then present its findings to the class, thus providing a range of different experiences which can be drawn on by the whole class throughout this unit.

Whatever students observe about the organisation of the business they investigate, it should be related to the nature of the product and its market.

Questions to be considered should include: how many different jobs are being done? To what extent are the people doing them different in terms of their skills and aptitudes? How are costs being reduced by having everyone specialise? This draws on previous work in Stage 1.

What decisions have been made recently? What does the management structure of the firm look like? What marketing strategies have been used?

Why is the business small, or relatively so? Where is its market? What sort of customers does it have? What would happen if it grew larger? What sort of competitors does it have? To what extent is it market-oriented? Why might it make sense for this business to stay small? These questions look forward towards the next few sections and, indeed, into the next unit.

It is possible to use a single local business investigation as the foundation for work on the whole of this and the next unit. If this is to be the strategy, read the advice for Investigation 2/2/1 on p. 26.

6 What happens when businesses grow?

Fixed and variable factors of production

Solid Plastics reappears here as a means of getting across some theoretical ideas which do not always fit neatly with the real world. Later on it is used again to give practice with cost calculations and to illuminate the idea of contribution. If you are able to get live data on costs from the industrial visit, and if these are not too confusing, comparisons could be very helpful.

The questions relating economies of scale to BP (6d) could be used as the basis for extended classroom discussion.

Do economies of scale apply to all kinds of business?

Here, too, there is scope for brainstorming, discussion and investigation of local business, considering the role of economies of scale and market orientation in a wide range of activities.

7 Efficiency and costs

Average, fixed and variable costs

Once students are familiar with the definitions, they can investigate the relationship between the different categories by calculating costs. However, they will need more practice in working with cost data than they will get from the *Student's Book* alone.

Some students may well point out that some costs are semi-variable. These are costs which are related to the level of output but are not directly proportional to it. They include the cost of power: some is used in the production process, but some is required for the offices and will be needed whatever the output. Other semi-variable costs are maintenance, marketing and administration. More maintenance tasks will need attention when output is high, but some will be needed even if production ceases temporarily. This has been left out of the *Student's Book*, because it will not be examined, but it should be talked over if it comes up in discussion.

It is important that students understand the purposes of both fixed and variable costs, and direct and indirect costs, and desirable that they understand the distinctions. It should be made very clear that they are different and separate approaches. Variable and direct costs should not be used together, or interchangeably, because they are not the same.

IT By this time students should ideally have acquired some proficiency in the use of spreadsheets. They could do Questions 7a on a spreadsheet, and investigate additional possibilities as well.

AC ❷ ❶ ❼ Activity: Tom Horsfield and his garage

This case study introduces some simple business jargon. If in doubt, students may need to look some things up in a business dictionary. It provides an introductory question on costs. It is a relatively straightforward case study and probably best omitted for abler students.

AC ❷ ❶ ❽ Activity: Anna's Aromatherapy

IT This is a very challenging exercise which might be better omitted with students who are not very confident.

The case study shows the ways in which costs can be

analysed. Again, both approaches to analysing costs can be used, although direct costs are not of great interest here because Anna has only one product. It would be possible to extend the exercise by introducing another possible product, say, beauty therapy of some sort. Direct costs and contribution can then be compared.

Costs can be presented on a spreadsheet.

Costing one extra unit
Marginal cost is introduced here because it is an important part of the marginal principle in economics and because it can figure in business decisions when there is a question of whether the firm should produce when the revenue will be insufficient to cover all its costs.

Average cost curves: do they all look the same?
This subsection is intended purely to make clear that individual firms will have very varied cost structures, depending on the product and the techniques of production. Again, it may be possible to relate this to local investigations.

8 Competition and technical efficiency

This section begins to draw the threads of the unit together. However, it is fairly brief because many

of the issues are dealt with in more detail in 'Do markets work?' (S2/3).

At no stage will it be necessary for students to study the standard diagram of perfect competition. The ideas can be used without the geometry.

9 Allocative efficiency

This section provides an explanation of how markets work when they are working reasonably well. This is important background for later work on market failure. It should help to explain recent political enthusiasm for markets and can be related to the work done in Stage 1 on privatisation.

❷❶❾ Investigation: Structural change
Students should investigate a current example of a structural change which is needed in order to move towards allocative efficiency. Any change which is the result of a shift in the pattern of demand would be suitable. It could be a declining industry which is shrinking due to lack of demand: bed and breakfast in seaside resorts, or any other inferior good. Or it could be a growing industry, perhaps associated with a new product or new technology. The best strategy may depend upon what is happening locally. The point is that resources should be moving into or out of the activity.

Stage 2: Unit 2 How do we increase efficiency?

The unit focuses on

- Investment appraisal
- Cash flow forecasting
- Credit control
- Stock control
- Just-in-time
- Kanban
- Human resource management
- Span of control
- Delayering
- Decentralisation
- Leadership styles
- Communication
- Improving allocative efficiency
- The costs and benefits of improved efficiency

Further ideas encountered

- Liquidity management
- Quality
- Market forces and distortions

General advice

This unit explores some of the ways in which efficiency can be improved through innovative business organisation. Inevitably, it has some weighty content.

It is very important that students realise that the success of measures to increase efficiency often depend on a whole package of different strategies being used together. In this unit, each section appears to be self-contained. In fact, students need to be able to integrate all the component parts of it when they come to take a problem-solving approach to business situations.

It is essential that students draw on their recent experiences and utilise their observations of local business. They should be able to see the links between what they are learning and what is happening at the present time within successful firms. As much as with 'What is efficiency?' (S2/1), students need industrial visits which they can use to put flesh upon the bones of the ideas they are learning. It may be possible to adopt an integrated approach to links with local business for the two units. This will encourage students to see and use the connections between the two units.

When we go beyond defining efficiency and begin to ask questions about how it can be improved, we are entering an area where there is a great deal of room for debate and sometimes controversy. Efficiency implies aims and objectives and these are not always obvious. There is scope for discussion, debate and role-play.

1 When should business invest?

In this section students are given a very brief introduction to investment, so that they can keep it in mind when considering a wide range of management strategies. Investment is explored further in Stage 3. It should be borne in mind that these methods of appraising investment give only a limited picture.

Questions 1b ask students to identify two local firms, one using labour-intensive, and the other capital-intensive, production methods. They should be able to recall the terms 'labour' and 'capital-intensive', and relate these to work done earlier on factor intensity.

2 Efficiency through quality

The objective here is to point up the link between quality and efficiency, and to ensure that, in subsequent sections, students are able to see quality control as a significant element in lean production.

Firms are often happy to talk about their quality control measures and the way in which these are integrated into the general management of production provides a good area for investigation. (See 2/2/1 below.)

3 Working capital management

Violette Ltd, the opening case study, uses the work done on the balance sheet in the last unit to explore a cash flow problem.

IT Students should have a rudimentary knowledge of cash flow from the work on 'How is a profit made?' (S1/2), which can now be developed further. The case study, Pershore Preserves, is a sizeable exercise for which about an hour may be needed. It could be the basis for a spreadsheet exercise.

The major clearing banks will supply useful specimen formats for cash-flow forecasts aimed at small business customers. These are worth collecting: the booklets also offer useful advice on working capital management.

❷❷❶ Investigation: A local business

Depending on what has already been done for 'What is efficiency?' (S2/1), students will need to investigate a local business. This should, if possible, be one which has recently made changes in order to enhance its efficiency. Students should construct their own questionnaire but may need help in ensuring that they are concentrating on the things that are going to be of concern throughout the unit. The following questions

may act as guidelines. Depending on the nature of the product, the questions will need to be adapted.

➤ What recent investment has there been? What was the thinking underlying the choice of technology?
➤ What quality control measures have been implemented?
➤ What stock control strategies are in operation?
➤ How have relationships with suppliers been developed?
➤ By what means does the business seek to respond quickly to changes in its market? When change is needed, how is it implemented?
➤ Have there been changes in the management structure? Why?

AC ❷❷❷ Activity: Greenwood and Co. Ltd

This is a further opportunity to work on a cash-flow forecast in a rather different context. The activity explores the link between cash and profit, which broadens the case theme to consider larger questions of efficiency.

4 Stock control and JIT

Situation 1 in the opening case study brings the stock-out problem close to home for students! They need to move from the idea of stock-out as 'bad luck' to recognition that it is either a calculated business risk or bad management.

Situation 2 is also a familiar enough scenario. Students should recognise the possible motives for the 'prices slashed' syndrome, distinguishing between stock with a low/falling net realisable value and a cash-flow crisis.

This scenario invites thought about the real business function of stock. The questions could act as a starting point for discussion of automated stock control and just-in-time techniques. Large chain-stores in the music business operate stock-control systems that are very sensitive to changes in high street demand.

Just-in-time

Given that many more firms are now pursuing lean production methods, it should be fairly easy to find a local firm where drastic reductions in stock turnover ratios can be seen and discussed. If possible, this work should be part of Investigation 2/2/1, and it could relate back to experiences the students have already had in connection with the previous unit. The importance of placing JIT in the context of lean production generally cannot be overstated.

The term kanban is often used in different ways. Here it is taken as referring to the Toyota card system, but with links to market orientation and pull-systems. The wider philosophy, incorporating quality assurance, JIT and market orientation, is gathered up in the paragraph on lean production.

AC ❷ ❷ ❸ Activity: JIT, Japan and the UK

Although not an easy piece from the student's point of view, this activity does provide some concrete evidence of the importance of JIT. It may be necessary to vary the questions to suit the group.

This activity uses 1988 data. If recent data are available locally, it may be possible to make comparisons and perhaps evaluate the extent of recent changes.

5 People: the greatest asset?

Up to this point the unit has been primarily concerned with production issues. It now turns to human resource management. Students have had a brief introduction to this in the previous unit where the reorganisation of BP figures as a case study, and where corporate culture has been touched upon.

Some time may be spent exploring the question of how the kind of culture change described in the case study 'Clotted Cream' affects job satisfaction and motivation. If there are appropriate local examples of culture change, then investigation of

this issue may be possible. Alternatively, the Toshiba experience might be compared with that of Burger King (2/2/4).

At the time of writing, the role of trade unions is under review by a House of Commons select committee. Some unions believe that they have a highly useful role to play in making UK manufacturing more competitive. All the major unions and the TUC have recorded their views and it would be worth gathering up-to-date information on this.

6 How should a firm be organised?

Students have been encouraged to think about the ways in which people are organised in two previous units, 'Why do people work?' (S1/1) and 'What is efficiency?' (S2/1). Once more they need to recall what they have already learnt. In particular, they should consider how elements of JIT, teamwork, a new corporate culture and a flatter, more decentralised management structure may be adopted in part or in various combinations as the business reacts to changes. Often the changes have been a response to painful situations resulting from increased competition or recession, or both.

AC ❷ ❷ ❹ Activity: Burger King

Burger King made drastic changes to their management structure after the merger with Wimpy. These made for much greater efficiency but had a high cost in terms of redundancies. This is a good opportunity for students to weigh up the pros and cons of delayering and decentralisation.

This activity starts as a simple comprehension exercise. It can be developed into a role play. In groups of three, students can take the roles of the Area Manager, the Restaurant Manager and a kitchen employee. They can focus first upon the problems they are facing as a result of the changes, and then compose a memo to HQ, outlining what needs to be done to deal with the problems.

AC ❷❷❺ Activity: Surprises

An opportunity to explore the effects of excessive centralisation.

7 Leadership

Students should link up this section with their earlier work on motivation. To a large extent the sections on organisations and hierarchies, and on leadership, form a co-ordinated whole, so that, at some stage, students need to develop an overview of this material.

❷❷❻ Activity: Reacting to different leadership styles

This is based on the opening case study in the *Student's Book*. Students can work in groups of three, each thinking out for themselves their own reaction to a manager of Type A, B or C. Then, as a group, they can draw up a profile of the kind of manager they feel they would respond to. This may well raise some gender issues which can usefully be explored.

AC ❷❷❼ Activity: The myth of leadership dismantled

This activity takes a fairly recent view of leadership. It can be contrasted with the more standard approach.

8 Communications

This section gives a quite brief survey of the importance of communication, which can be greatly enhanced if Activity 2/2/8 is used also.

AC ❷❷❽ Activity: Employee participation

These data were collected in 1990. They should alert students to one aspect of communication and how it

may have improved in local firms as a result of similar recent measures.

This starts as a data interpretation exercise but could be extended by using it as a basis for a debate of the issues involved. Alternatively, it could be the start of an investigation of local experience in this field.

9 Improving allocative efficiency

This section ties in to 'What is efficiency?' (S2/1) and also has links with the next unit. There is some emphasis on the nature of optimal allocation but without any reference to the full rigour of the 'Pareto' analysis. It would be useful to explore the gap between theory and 'reality' in the classroom and to discuss the relevance of the theory in giving predictions about the efficacy of markets.

Perfect competition is dealt with here. The objective is to ensure that students can see why markets have advantages as a means of allocation, without introducing the formal diagrammatic treatment which would be inappropriate on this course.

AC ❷❷❾ Activity: Party Products Ltd

This activity provides a situation where the student has the opportunity to reflect on how resources are allocated via the price mechanism. This should put some of the theory into a rather more concrete context and enable the student to engage with the idea that factor movements might be tending towards 'desirable' or optimal solutions, without overt administrative control. It is recommended that the teacher use this case study to initiate discussion of a wider nature, e.g. markets may be efficient but what about the issues of equity and fairness; does a market always produce 'correct' solutions? The moral dimension and the idea of market failure can be introduced here.

It should be made clear that to produce unwanted goods and services is a waste of productive resources which might be better used elsewhere.

Ways of using the case study

➤ Suggest that the students role-play the scene where Danielle and Jane have to lay off their workers and explore the feelings of workers and directors (contrast market efficiency with the personal human cost).

➤ Propose the idea that Danielle and Jane should simply have sold up, sold the assets and paid back the bank. Should they have done that? Are there reasons other than the financial ones for people running companies?

➤ Role-play the interview between Danielle and the bank manager (construct some simple accounts figures) when the bank wants its loan back. This could be a good opening to discuss the role of the banks – are they 'fair-weather friends'; do they do a reasonable job? Some statistics on company failures/bankruptcies might be useful to this discussion.

Reallocating capital

When you feel that students are happy with the idea of market allocation, and have read the *Student's Book* section on capital markets, you could try Activity 2/2/10.

❷❷⑩ Activity: A stock market

➤ Divide some students into (about) six companies. Ask them to stand on one side of the room with a large, poster-sized sheet of paper.

➤ Remaining students are 'investors'. Ask two or three students to be observers. The investors' job is to buy shares in the company they think best.

➤ Nominate someone to roll the dice (use two dice). The resulting score is the return on assets for the companies. This is rolled for each company in turn – the ROA is written up on their poster.

➤ Make sure each company has only 'x' shares to sell – in other words far fewer than the likely demand if all the investors want them from one particular company (e.g. about 4 per company if there are 24 investors and 6 companies). State categorically that all shares are being offered at the same price (provide the investors with enough 'cash' to buy at least one share each).

➤ Shout out 'at the word "Go", purchase shares in the company/ies you feel will benefit you most – "GO!"'

The running about, heated discussion and general chaos which should ensue can be likened later to the conditions which really do prevail in the markets! When the dust has settled, discuss the lessons to be learnt from the situation – how has the financial market ensured that the most efficient firms obtained the investment they required? Ask the observers to report back – did some companies have excess demand for their shares – why? Did some companies find fewer interested (and no doubt some disgruntled) investors? Analyse why the successful companies sold out their shares first, and lead the discussion (or indeed the game if you feel up to it) on to what would happen to the various share prices when a secondhand market starts.

9 Efficiency in what?

At this point students should give consideration to the costs of the long–term drive for efficiency. This section foreshadows the discussion of externalities in the next unit.

Stage 2: Unit 3 Do markets work?

The unit focuses on

- Elasticity: price, income, cross, marketing
- Monopoly
- Oligopoly
- Game theory
- Cartels
- Price discrimination
- Advertising
- Externalities
- Market failure

Further ideas encountered

- The effect of changes in the economy on industry
- Cost benefit analysis

General advice

There is a wide range of activities in this guide. Some of them are classroom-based, small-scale activities. Others are much larger in scope and time consumption. There are often several activities which deal with the same section. The aim is that you should be able to select the type of activity that is appropriate for your circumstances or invent your own and let us know about them. It would be impossible to carry out all the activities in the time available. The first sections of this unit are concerned with the understanding of elasticity. The ideas of basic supply and demand have already been laid down in 'How is a profit made?' (S1/2) and should now be picked up for further elucidation.

The unit also covers the main section of work to be done on the theory of the firm. It builds on the work on perfect competition in 'What is efficiency?' (S2/1) and deals with monopoly and oligopoly without entering into a geometric explanation. Profit-payoff matrices are a useful way of

demonstrating why some forms of competition are more effective in producing greater efficiency in the allocation of resources. Students can readily follow their workings through the prisoner's dilemma exercise (2/3/10).

The final part of the unit looks at market failure. The motor industry is a good vehicle for this topic because, initially, it seems to work rather well but, on closer inspection, students will readily tell you how it fails. These and other, more general, failures are drawn together at the end of the unit, where the attempts to rectify them are briefly discussed.

1 How the market responds to change

This section puts to work the ideas of supply and demand that were initially encountered in Stage 1. Students are asked to consider just how shifts in demand take place. This introduces the idea that the market is dynamic rather than static.

IT Question 1a/4 asks students to use the Nuffield Investigations and Data disk to test the response of car buyers to changes in the state of the economy. This could be done by comparing total sales with variables such as national income or unemployment.

❷❸❶ Investigation: The car market: supply and demand

Students can gain an understanding of how the car market operates by considering the following changes and their effect on the car market:

1 An end to an economic recession in the UK.
2 A large increase in the subsidies paid to public transport.

3 Abolition of import quotas on Japanese cars.
4 A massive increase in the price of petrol due to a crisis in the Middle East.

In each case they should draw a demand and supply diagram and

1 Predict whether the change will affect demand or supply.
2 Predict whether the demand or supply increases or decreases. How is this shown on the diagram?
3 Predict the effect on price and quantity consumed.

This can be developed further by an investigation of the effect the current economic situation is having on the car market.

Such an investigation, carried out in terms of students' knowledge of demand and supply, would make a useful contribution to the portfolio.

2 How the consumer responds to change

Elasticity is introduced in this section. It is worth reminding students that the divisor is always the *original* price and quantity.

AC ❷ ❸ ❷ Activity: Income and price elasticity of demand

This activity requires students to estimate income elasticities for a range of simple products, and then price elasticities for comparison.

During discussion, students should be able to draw out the reasons for the differences in elasticities. They can use the data provided as a basis for their estimates.

❷ ❸ ❸ Investigation: A price elasticity survey

Manufacturers believe that cheaper cars are more price elastic than expensive cars. This survey gives students the opportunity to test this as a hypothesis.

Select a range of potential car purchasers (probably adults, if the answers are going to be useful) and ask them whether they would be prepared to buy a car at a given range of prices, for example:

Metro 1.1S	Rover 420 GSi
£7,500	£13,500
£7,750	£13,750
£8,000	£14,000
£8,250	£14,250
£8,500	£14,500
£8,750	£14,750
£9,000	£15,000

Choose any make of car that you feel is appropriate and update prices as necessary.

3 Why is elasticity important to businesses?

This section completes the introduction to elasticity. It investigates the relationship between elasticity and revenue and shows the relevance of cross elasticities and marketing elasticity. The latter is used as it covers the whole of the marketing function. It is pointed out that any sub-set of marketing, such as advertising, can be treated in the same way. Elasticity is important to businesses although they may not always use the terminology. This section aims to demonstrate how.

Question 3b/1 in the *Student's Book* asks where the price increase should fall on two products with different elasticities. Students should recognise that with a price elasticity of 1.2, increasing the price will lead to a more than proportionate fall in demand so the companies' revenue will fall. If the price elasticity is 0.8, the fall in demand will be proportionately less than the rise in price, so revenue will fall.

In order to check that this is understood in different contexts and with different figures, it is worth using a range of different products with different elasticities.

AC ❷❸❹ Activity: Elasticity along a demand curve

This is a numerical exercise to show how the price elasticity of demand varies along a straight demand curve and the implications of this for changes in price and the consequent effect on revenue.

❷❸❺ Activity: Substitutes and complements

In groups or pairs, students can consider the impact on the sale of cars of a change in price of the following products:

➤ Price of other transport
➤ Secondhand cars
➤ Petrol
➤ Servicing and maintenance costs

The concept can then be tested by asking students to identify other non-motor industry products and considering their impact when price changes. Because petrol was used as an example in 1/2/4, there is some danger of cars and petrol being brought in too much. It is a particularly good complement example but teachers may want to drop it now!

4 Competition in the market

Perfect competition was introduced in 'What is efficiency?' (S2/1). The theme is picked up and developed here. Perfect competition and monopoly are explained as reference points but without the traditional geometry. It is important that students realise that they are the ends of the spectrum and that most markets fall somewhere in between. The degree of competition in the motor industry is used to identify the range of competition and the limitations created by the market. The need for control of monopoly, because of the power it gives to companies to restrict output or control price and therefore make supernormal profit, is

introduced. The purpose of the Monopolies and Mergers Commission is discussed.

AC ❷❸❻ Activity: The spectrum of competition

This activity requires students to place a range of product markets on the spectrum, having regard to the questions, which should help them to judge the industries appropriately.

5 Oligopoly and competition

Oligopoly is covered in some detail as it is the market structure which is most frequently encountered. The profit pay-off matrix is used as a method of evaluating different market structures. The idea of the pp matrix is quite straightforward and is developed by several exercises which follow.

Discussion of price discrimination gives us the opportunity to investigate the workings of the car market.

❷❸❼ Investigation: The UK car market is an example of an oligopolistic market

Students should examine this hypothesis by gathering data on the UK car industry and testing the extent to which these data conform to the characteristics of oligopolistic markets outlined in the section. (This investigation may be linked with Investigation 2/3/11.)

Data could be gathered on:
➤ current market shares of major manufacturers
➤ advertising by the main companies
➤ brochures produced by these companies
➤ prices being offered for similar makes of car.

IT This exercise can also be performed using the Nuffield Investigations and Data disk. There is an exercise in the supporting material which uses concentration ratios to analyse the market. It could be carried out for any appropriate industry for which data are available.

AC ❷❸❽ Activity: Do consumers pay more for cars in the UK than in the rest of Europe?

This activity is designed to identify the characteristics of price discrimination and to assist students to demonstrate their understanding in the context of the car market.

❷❸❾ Activity: An oligopoly game

The aim of the activity is to explore the way companies operate in oligopolistic markets. The importance of interdependence and the conflicting pressures of co-operation and competition can be raised, as well as issues such as price stickiness.

The class should be split up into groups of two or three; each group represents an industry and each individual student a firm within that industry.

The aim of each company is to make profits and the winner is the company with the greatest profit after an agreed number of rounds.

In each period the company must decide what price to charge for its product (high, medium or low). Before making their decision, companies may discuss what price each should charge, but any agreements are not binding – the final decision on what price to charge is taken separately and secretly.

Cheating *is* allowed!

After prices have been set they are revealed and the appropriate level of sales each company has made in that period is recorded. Using the data provided, calculate the profit or loss the company has made in that period and then add or subtract this profit or loss to or from the running total.

Profit = sales revenue – total costs

Sales revenue = price x quantity sold

Total costs = fixed costs + variable costs (average variable cost x quantity sold)

After an agreed number of rounds, students should

consider some of the following relevant issues which may have

Who won? Why was their strate this strategy work again? Was collusion? How were such deals carried out and maintained? Why did deals sometimes not succeed? Was there a price war? Did anyone benefit? Did you arrive at a stable outcome? If so what was the outcome and why was it stable?

What have we learned about the possible behaviour patterns of firms in oligopolistic industries?

Oligopoly game: running details

Aim	To maximise profits
Assumptions	Fixed costs are £1000 per month
	Variable costs are 20p per unit produced
Price options	High (H) – 80p
	Medium (M) – 60p
	Low (L) – 40p

Outcomes

Price combination	Price decision	Sales
H H H	H	3,000
H H L	H	0
	L	13,000
H H M	H	0
	M	10,000
H M L	H	0
	M	2,100
	L	11,000
H M M	H	0
	M	5,500
H L L	H	0
	L	6,600
M M M	M	3,800
M M L	M	2,000
	L	9,300
M L L	M	400
	L	6,500
L L L	L	4,500

⑩ Activity: The prisoner's dilemma

The aims of this activity are:
1 To explore the profit pay-off matrix in more detail.
2 To highlight the conflict between competition and co-operation which is inherent in oligopoly.

Students should be placed in groups of three (one is to play the role of judge and the other two are to be prisoners, Blue and Green). The student playing the role of judge reads out the following scenario to the two prisoners:

The words of the judge:
> '... because neither of you is prepared to confess to this crime, I am going to give both of you one year in jail. However, if one of you will confess, I will reduce your sentence to three months while your partner will get ten years. If you both confess than I will give you both a sentence of five years each.'

The two prisoners may confer but must give their decision to the judge separately.

After the exercise, students should consider the following questions:
1 Draw the appropriate profit pay-off matrix.
2 What was the final position you reached and why?
3 In what ways is this situation similar to, and different from, a firm in an oligopolistic market?
4 What do you understand by the idea of interdependence and how does this influence the behaviour of firms in oligopoly?

❷❸⑪ Investigation: How do firms compete?

Using the material gained in Activity 2/3/7, students can list and analyse the various techniques being used by car companies to attract consumers to buy their car, or other product, rather than a competitor's car.

Students can also consider the extent to which these techniques vary in importance over time.

❷❸⑫ Activity/Investigation: Price discrimination

Based on quotes from various interested parties, students can discuss the extent to which there is evidence of price discrimination in the UK car market or whether the price differential which exists between UK cars and those in Europe can be explained by other factors.

In this way students should gain a clearer understanding of price discrimination and how difficult it is to prove in practice.

This can be followed up by research to identify other products where price discrimination occurs. Some real examples with details of the theoretical explanations of how the conditions are demonstrated in each case would make a good portfolio entry.

6 Advertising: temptation and persuasion

Section 6 investigates advertising: why it is done, what it costs, controls and exploitation.

AC ❷❸⑬ Activity/investigation: Advertising cars

Students should undertake some market research on car advertising. In groups they could explore different aspects of the topic.
➤ One group could undertake a panel session looking at current attitudes to advertising using a cross section of consumers.
➤ A second group could draw up a questionnaire examining the factors people see as important when choosing a car.
➤ Another group could examine the techniques used by car companies to advertise their product and how these have changed over the years.
➤ A final group could attempt to put the ideas of persuasion to work. The photocopiable sheet relating to this activity contains a story board for a futile American attempt to relaunch the Yugo! Can the students do better?

7 The environment: paying the price

Private costs, externalities and social costs are the main theme of this section. These are looked at through the issues of pollution and congestion and how to control them. The profit-payoff matrix is used to explain why firms continue to pollute if there is no legislation. Students are asked to consider the costs and benefits of alternative strategies.

AC ❷ ❸ ⓮ Activity: Traffic congestion in Farnham

This activity is based on a genuine problem faced by a community that has severe problems of congestion. It has been particularly well documented and is open to public consultation.

Students are asked to use the ideas that they have encountered in the chapter to weigh up alternative strategies.

If there is a similar problem in your locality, use it instead as it will provide greater immediacy and relevance.

Stage 3: Unit 1 How do firms expand?

The unit focuses on

- Growth and the firm
- Sources of finance
- The marketing mix
- Market segmentation
- New product development
- Product life cycle and portfolio
- Mergers and takeovers
- Capital structures

Further ideas encountered

- Measurement of size and growth in firms
- Market research
- SWOT analysis
- Diversification and focus
- Research and development
- Long-run average costs
- Change management

General advice

The unit builds directly and strongly on work done in Stage 2. The broad theme of expansion is explored through the natural tendency of firms to grow, subject to constraints such as time, place and risk. Extending the analogy of new business as seedcorn, there is an assumption that firms, like seeds, will grow in the favourable conditions that it is their nature to seek out. Although there is a strong emphasis on business opportunity and the pro-active management of change, there is also recognition that firms have periods of contraction or consolidation and that mere survival may sometimes be the best interpretation of growth.

Market forces are the basic context for this unit and provide its theoretical underpinning. Students should extend their awareness of the market's allocative power and the sense in which business expansion is an increasing demand on scarce resources that carry a very tangible opportunity cost. They should also apply their understanding of the price mechanism to the process of achieving sales. It is important to appreciate the dual focus on producer and consumer. Producers strive to widen the gap between costs and market value, while consumers aim to maximise their surplus through the difference between expenditure and satisfaction.

This analysis should give the unit an interesting conceptual rationale. It should also highlight the power of a joint approach to economics and business, making many connections which the separate subjects do not make obvious. Indeed, this should not be perceived or taught as a 'business studies' unit. Although there is a good deal of material on business management and behaviour, there is a continuous need to apply microeconomic theory if issues are to be explored properly.

There is a substantial amount of material relating to marketing in this unit. This is consistent as it is only through effective marketing that most firms are able to expand. However, the unit is not intended to 'cover' marketing as in a conventional business studies syllabus. Markets and marketing are simply a key dimension to understanding the phenomenon of growth. As in all parts of the course, they should be studied in an integrated context. The application of economic theory to marketing is clearly most important. Developing ideas first encountered in 'How is a profit made?', (S1/2), the aim is to explore beneath the external features of marketing behaviour to reveal its meaning and coherence.

Finance is important to this unit but it should not be approached as an end in itself. As a way of quantifying resource implications, finance can be woven through the teaching as a useful language of enquiry.

Finally, in terms of content, it is essential to keep the theme of business organisation and human resources alive. It is people who drive the expansion of firms but it is also often people who are the greatest source of constraint. The human realities of business decision making should constantly be stressed.

Plenty of contentious issues are likely to arise in studying this unit. As always, these are to be welcomed and will, we hope, generate subjects for debate. The 'bigness' of business is a lively topic, while the ethics of marketing tactics are always open to question. The theme of business expansion may even prompt argument about the merits of a 'consumer society', with its implications for both the environment and human values.

1 An expanding firm

This unit introduces students to the reality of business expansion and explores ways of measuring the speed and extent of its growth. There should be some current company annual reports available for reference and illustrative purposes. The subject of capitalisation can be pursued using the *Financial Times* share prices page that appears on a Monday – other quality papers also print capitalisation data on Mondays, e.g. *The Independent. The Times 1000* is a very useful reference book throughout.

Questions 1a could make a group activity in class. Question 1 might be enjoyable as an introductory brainstorm. The other questions are partly speculative but encourage consideration of the issues that are to follow.

Questions 1b develop understanding of nominal and real prices. This is clearly an important idea and many students find it confusing. Question 3

picks up the accounting thread from Stage 2. It may be worth running through some quick revision of key accounting concepts at this point. The data for the stimulus material used here could be updated by requesting a latest annual report from Cadbury-Schweppes (group headquarters: 1 Connaught Place, London W2 2EX. Tel. 0171-262 1212).

Questions 1c could be extended by examining some real examples of firms where judgements of relative size depend on criteria chosen.

There are two sets of Open Questions in this section. The first ones need divergent thinking and lend themselves to discussion. The second set provides a chance to discuss some of the ethical issues raised by business expansion in general and the expansion of certain industries in particular.

❸ ❶ ❶ Investigation: Expansion profiles

Over the course of this unit, the students could prepare an expansion profile for one firm of their choice. In practice, most firms carry some story of expansion. Some are gradual over quite long periods of history, while others are dramatic and recent. It is important to include reference to non-profit-making organisations, such as pressure groups, charities and clubs/societies. Where relevant, a school or college is an entirely valid example and could provide rich evidence.

Some interesting 'classic' examples include: Virgin, Amstrad, Habitat (now owned by Ikea), Sainsbury's, Glaxo, GEC, British Airways, Dixons, EMAP publishing, Body Shop, MFI Furniture, Kwik-Fit, Land Securities, Saachi and Saachi, etc. A trade union (e.g. Manufacturing, Science and Finance) or a charity (e.g. Oxfam) would also be good choices.

A local story of expansion can be just as revealing – more so if a manager or owner is willing to co-operate. Confidentiality of accounting information can be a problem.

The activity will be most useful if an excessively descriptive approach is avoided. Some lines of enquiry that could be fruitful include:

➤ When and why was the business founded?

➤ Were there any turning points for expansion and why?

➤ What factors have driven growth?

➤ What factors have constrained growth?

➤ How has expansion been financed?

➤ To what extent have staff numbers increased?

➤ Has the firm grown more or less than others in the same industry/area? Reasons?

➤ What problems have been created by growth? How are these being resolved?

When the students' individual or group studies are complete, some comparison may be possible. In particular, it would be interesting to look for common elements in the 'expansion experience'. This could be an item for the portfolio.

❸❶❷ Investigation: Company financial analysis

This activity gives the student some practice in extracting and handling financial data. A wider growth survey across a number of firms in the same or different sectors would have potential as an element of portfolio work. The use and meaning of the constant purchasing power conversion table may need highlighting for some students (this is in the *Data Book*). Question 2 simply requires the calculation of a percentage which can then be added to 100 to give the index number. Question 4 builds on the material in Stage 2. Question 5 must make use of specific numerate evidence with percentage changes etc. You may wish to adapt the investigation to suit particular requirements.

Student tasks

Take the annual report and accounts of any public company. (If you do not have an annual report available, write to, or telephone, a firm of your choice and request a copy.) Find the chairman's statement which usually appears in the first few pages. See if it makes any reference to the scale or growth of the firm. Then turn to the formal accounts and see if you can verify such references. Find the group 'financial record' (or equivalent) which usually provides accounting data over five consecutive years.

1 Construct a segmented bar-chart to illustrate changes to sales and operating profit over the years for which you have found data.

2 Construct a simple index for the same data series with base year = 100, using the earliest year for this. The index can be calculated for each year by taking the percentage change and adding it to 100.

3 Now deflate the money data using the conversion table in the *Data Book* to make the conversions.

4 Analyse changes in total assets less current liabilities and comment on any relationship with sales and profit.

5 In your judgement, to what extent, if any, has the firm expanded over the period? Do you have any comments to make on the chairman's statement? Use the accounting data to provide evidence.

2 Why do firms grow?

A real attempt should be made to answer this question. It is a complex issue and is a matter of assessing and balancing different explanations. The idea of the price mechanism as a way of understanding growth is important.

Questions 2a relate to a classic 1980s growth story. Many students will have views on the subject, which could be the impetus for discussion. George Davies is a very interesting business personality and worth researching. The near collapse of the Next empire in 1990 is a good example of decline and contraction. The Next Annual Reports are very revealing, changing from lavish 'designer' publications in the late 1980s to diminutive and rather pathetic formal statements in the 1990s! (The company is quite helpful in supplying such material: Next plc, Desford Road, Enderby, Leicester LE9 5AT. Tel. (01533) 866411.) The firm's recovery and qualified resumption of growth is a fascinating outcome. Also very interesting is the share price which slumped to an all-time low of 9p in December 1990 only to become the perfect recovery stock over the following three years.

IT Further investigation of the clothing industry is possible using the Nuffield Investigations and Data disk.

Questions 2b could best be illustrated by local examples, e.g. traditional retailers or small service-based sole traders and partnerships.

Questions 2c are a chance to look again at consumer surplus and then to introduce the power of marketing.

Open Questions in this section focus on the human motives for expansion and can be related to career ambitions. The significance of money and power as business motives may spark an interesting discussion.

3 Analysing markets

The unit explores the meaning of market orientation and returns briefly to market research. Techniques of market segmentation are then examined, leading to the concept of market positioning. An abundance of evidence for this area exists in the media and in any high street. Students may also have part-time jobs or work experience that is relevant. Magazines such as *Campaign* or *Marketing Week* are valuable in giving the flavour of the marketing world – back numbers can often be obtained free from advertising or marketing agencies (try *Yellow Pages*).

Questions 3a are quite difficult but lead students to think carefully about market research findings and to recognise that the 'experts' can be very wrong.

Questions 3b reintroduce the theme of opportunity cost and prompt thought about the nature of purchasing decisions.

Questions 3c return to the theme of demand and price. The questions could work well as a discussion agenda, perhaps with some advance preparation.

AC ❸ ❶ ❸ Investigation and activity: The market for organic food

The section on market research builds on the introduction given in 'How is a profit made?' (S1/2). It is possible to return to the theme of organic food for this market research activity. Alternatively, the activity could be adapted for other products.

This investigation involves the students in formulating their own hypotheses concerning the market for organic food. These can then be tested, using field research, and appropriate conclusions drawn. The process should provide some basic experience of market research techniques and the results may be revealing about how the chosen market is segmented.

Students could work in pairs or small groups. It may be useful to set a broad agenda for an open discussion. Issues that could be raised include:
➤ Nature of the relevant market segment
➤ Consumer motives
➤ Price and price changes
➤ Income and availability
➤ Distribution patterns
➤ Background of increased concern regarding health and diet
➤ Environmental and ethical aspects to modern agriculture.

IT They should then discuss the investigation and frame one or more hypotheses. They must decide on a strategy for testing their hypotheses. This is likely to involve a survey of some kind using a questionnaire. Any sampling method used should be carefully chosen and justified. The Nuffield Investigations and Data disk may be useful in providing background information, e.g. changes in real incomes. Students on maths/statistics courses may be able to apply a significance test but this is not an expectation.

The investigation might end with a review of the results obtained. It is important that students are critical of their own methods. They should appreciate that real market research is a use of scarce resources, with its scope and level of accuracy needing a commercial justification.

❸❶❹ Activity: Orientating to the market

Market orientation is literally an orientation of mind-set. It is, in essence, a simple idea, yet its applications are not always obvious and can be very subtle. The last ten years have seen a shift of focus from product to market for many organisations in the public as well as the private sector. The activity on this theme involves analysing the output of an organisation in terms of:

a) the producer and the product
b) the consumer and the market.

For example, a product-orientated view of BT would stress cables, connections, switchgear, telephones and faxes. A market-orientated view would be more concerned with family, friends, news, efficiency, convenience and style.

Students could use a simple grid to analyse product- and market-orientated understandings of output for the industries below. Alternatively, they could work in pairs or small groups to build more complete pictures, with a short presentation to the whole class.

Suggested industries

➤ Burglar alarms
➤ Bicycles
➤ Parcel post
➤ Home insurance
➤ Building societies' savings accounts

❸❶❺ Investigation: Gaps in the market

The idea is for students to identify 'gaps in the market' and to suggest how they might be filled. This will draw together the ideas in this section and also open the way towards new product development in Section 4. The length of the activity depends very much on teacher

choice. It could simply involve a few minutes' discussion of apparent absences of products in particular industries. Equally pairs/groups of students could carry out market research to find a 'gap', illustrate this with a 2-criteria segmentation map and describe the qualities and appeal of a proposed product in a report to the whole class. This could be based on students using a flip chart or OHP transparency, or it could be written up in a short report.

It might first be worth discussing the meaning of the term 'a gap in the market' using a simple segmentation diagram.

4 Product development

The unit covers the basic ideas in NPD and students should be able to think of many examples. It could be worth beginning with a general brainstorm on products introduced in the last 3/5/10+ years. These can be divided among generic products, brands and brand variants. Students should consider services as well as consumer goods and be reminded of the capital goods sector. The product life cycle is introduced and this can be quickly linked to the idea of a product portfolio. Students should remember that these are text book models and that real situations are rarely so neat. Finally, SWOT analysis draws attention to the dynamic nature of competitive markets where even a successful product can quickly be eclipsed by another innovation or change in the total business environment.

Questions 4a relate to a classic product and marketing success that most students will recognise. Further information on this amazing story can be found in *Alan Sugar* by David Thomas (Pan, 1990).

Questions 4b stress the issue of dynamism in markets. The students may be able to think of local firms that did not 'rock the boat' – and the consequences.

Questions 4c represent a short case study which illustrates the difficulties in interpreting the product life cycle.

Questions 4d is a simple Boston Matrix problem. It would probably be useful for the students to draw the scenario first to gain familiarity with the idea.

IT The Nuffield Investigations and Data disk has information relating to the recorded music industry, which can be used to investigate the product life cycle in the context of CDs, cassettes and vinyl.

5 Increasing sales

This section shows how firms attempt to increase sales through the marketing mix. The approach aims to emphasise the integrated nature of the mix and to avoid the over-simplistic 4Ps approach. The idea of price and benefits as the determining influences on sales is explained through joint use of business and micro-economic concepts. The area is again rich in accessible case study resources and much useful teaching material can be found in the press, in periodicals and on video.

Questions 5a link the market positioning thread to the concept of a marketing mix. It could make an interesting start to the session by asking students to scribble down their associations with the Lucozade brand.

Questions 5c illustrate the important, but often overlooked, principle that exploitation of price elasticity to increase revenue does not necessarily lead to increased profitability – indeed, profit is a quite different concept. This elasticity fallacy finds vigorous application in fast-moving consumer goods markets, e.g. in supermarkets' special offers.

Some discussion of advertising ethics is desirable at this stage. This could focus on the honesty and

decency of ads (useful material from ASA) and also on such wider questions as the impact of advertising on children, the ability of consumers to make sensible and informed judgements, the promotion of harmful products, the role of advertising in inflating material expectations, etc, etc.

AC ③ ① ⑥ Activity: Baxters of Speyside

An introductory survey of student perceptions relative to this brand would make an interesting start. A 'prop', e.g. a tin of Royal Game Soup, would add interest and focus. Question 1 raises the issue of intuitive/scientific decision making, which remains contentious. The market positioning map should be drawn on criteria of socio-economic grade and age-group of consumers. Question 4 anticipates Section 7 but students should be able to discuss the debt/risk factor.

AC ③ ① ⑦ Activity: Yorkie

This is a classic marketing case study which, although relating to the 1970s, continues to generate high student interest. The introduction of the material is important and teachers could usefully use their own memory to supply some anecdotal evidence ...? Being able to pass around a few examples of the product adds realism and student interest! The Channel 4 Series *The Marketing Mix* (1988) featured Yorkie and is worth using if available.

This activity is more time-consuming and depends on good 'staging'. The 'parts' structure is important, adding pace and surprise to events. Students need to work in small groups and a plenary discussion at the end of each part would be valuable. The price/value survey in Part 4 could either involve some primary research, or samples could be brought into the classroom – but their weights and prices need careful advance checking.

6 Mergers and take-overs

This unit is a brief survey of business integration and its control. It builds on prior knowledge from Stage 2, from which students should have a basic understanding of market structures and the problem of monopoly. The European and international dimensions of this subject need constant stress and there is real scope for debate (see 3/1/8).

Questions 6a highlight the recurrent debate over the case for horizontal integration as a means to compete in international markets. Current and archive press material on this subject is always valuable and any bid in progress is worth debate.

Questions 6c address the trend away from diversification towards corporate focus. At the time of writing (mid 1993), the Hanson saga continues and might be compared with the comparable success of Williams Brothers. Again, press material is useful. The subject of divestment is topical in the 1990s and makes a good link to management buy-outs.

Questions 6d explore the famous advice from Peters and Waterman. The theme has become increasingly important, with high-profile examples such as ICI and Zeneca. Ideally, students should read at least part of *In Search of Excellence* (Harper Collins, 1982), perhaps with some discussion to follow.

❸❶❽ Activity: Mock Monopolies and Mergers Commission bid referral

A simple simulation of an MMC referral, hearing and decision will highlight the major issues in a bid situation and reveal the difficult criteria that the Commission attempts to apply. A short video is available from the MMC, 48 Carey Street, London WC2A 2JT (price £10).

The powers of the MMC are defined under Section 84 of the Fair Trading Act, 1973. Members are appointed by the President of the Board of Trade and serve for renewable three-year terms. It is worth stressing the human realities of the MMC: its members are mainly part-time, seconded industrialists, lawyers, academics and trade unionists who try to assess the merits of very complex cases. Each referral is considered by a panel of four, five or six people plus the chair. Experts can be added to the team and there is a permanent staff to advise and assist. The MMC

has extensive legal powers, e.g. to subpoena witnesses, but in practice these are rarely, if ever, used.

Each side in a merger referral attends hearings at which they can present their position. The decision to recommend allowing or blocking the bid depends mainly on the likely implications for competition in the industry and how this will affect the public interest. The relevant arena for competition is no longer purely domestic and a European context has become increasingly important. Factors outside the immediate issue of competition can also be considered. Regional and employment implications may be important. If the MMC finds the merger is not against the public interest, the merger is allowed to proceed. If it is against the public interest, the MMC recommends to the President of the Board of Trade that the merger should not be allowed. He then decides whether to accept the recommendation. If he accepts the recommendation, he can then seek undertakings from the parties involved.

A class simulation might take an actual case, such as Rowntree/Nestlé, or an imaginary scenario, such as a bid by Mars for Cadbury-Schweppes or by Cadbury-Schweppes for Thorntons. A useful publication (available free from Cadbury's at Bournville, Birmingham B30 2LU. Tel. 0121-458 2000) is their *Chocolate Market Review* for the current year, with details of relative market shares, value of sectors, segments, etc. Clearly, the students could not enter into the technical details of a bid but could present simply the main pros and cons with some supporting evidence. Real bids can be researched quite easily using press analysis from the time. The Rowntree takeover is included in *Business Case Studies* by Ian Marcousé and David Lines (Longman, 1990).

7 Financing expansion

The section tackles the financial aspects of expansion, examining internal and external sources of funds. The numeracy demands are very straightforward but there is scope for interested students to pursue more advanced work. It is important for the students to appreciate that gaining and keeping control of resources always carries an opportunity cost. For public companies in particular, there is a continuous requirement to demonstrate efficiency and relative success.

Open Questions raise the issue of government support for industry, which should stimulate discussion. Question 4 opens up a deceptively large and complex debate.

8 Managing expansion

Questions 8a relate to a simple storyline, but Question 4 needs careful thought with stress on human factors extending into Question 5.

AC ❸ ❶ ❾ Activity: Satisfying Mrs Jones

This case study integrates a good deal of earlier material in addressing the problems faced by a famous multinational seeking to expand. Further information is readily available from Unilever plc, Unilever House, Blackfriars, London EC1. The 'Mrs Jones' theme is worth exploring as it captures so precisely the idea of market orientation.

Stage 3: Unit 2 What makes an economy grow?

The unit focuses on

- Economic growth
- Aggregate demand
- Aggregate supply
- Circular flow
- National income and its components
- Sources of growth
- The role of innovation, investment, cultural change, education, government
- Supply side economics
- Production possibility frontiers
- Data interpretation
- Costs and benefits of growth

Further ideas encountered

- Corporate culture
- Inflation
- Structural change
- Government's economic influence
- Competitiveness
- Multinationals
- Trade
- Tariffs and quotas
- Sustainable growth
- Environmental accounting

General advice

At the beginning of the unit, you could ask students to collect newspaper articles which discuss events in the economy, environmental damage which is occurring, benefits accruing to a country, firm or individual, or examples of how firms or economies are growing anywhere in the world. Various activities in this unit will use them as a basis for further work.

The unit focuses on growth as it affects both developing and developed countries. It provides an opportunity to explore basic macro-economic theory using aggregate demand and supply, while building on ideas that have been established in the previous units.

The relationship between growth in the micro- and the macroeconomy is shown through case studies of businesses and a discussion of their impact on the economy as a whole. It is important that students realise that growth is not just an abstract phenomenon which is achieved by governments but is, rather, the summation of business activity working in an environment created by government.

Students are asked to consider whether growth is always 'good'. The idea of environmental accounting is introduced as a method of evaluating the costs of growth.

The final section asks whether there are any lessons that the UK can learn from the experience of others.

1 What is economic growth?

Section 1 starts to build the basic theoretical framework for the unit. The concept of aggregate supply and how it can be used to demonstrate growth is introduced. Japan is used as a case study.

❸❷❶ Activity: What do we know about Japan?

Brainstorming on Japan. No precise knowledge of the Japanese economy is expected. However, students should be aware that Japan is a successful exporter of manufactured products and is often more competitive than UK manufacturers. They might also be able to cite inward investment into the UK, such as Toyota at Derby and Nissan at Sunderland, as examples of Japanese success. Better students will be able to analyse what might be meant by an economic 'miracle'.

AC ❸❷❷ Activity: War, defence and economic growth

This activity could be done in groups or in written form at home. Students should identify the destruction of factors of production arising from war and should analyse the effect this has on the productive potential of the economy. They should also be able to appreciate that while war may destroy much of the physical capital of an economy, human capital is less likely to be destroyed to the same extent. Hence, economies which, in the past, have had relatively high levels of human capital before a war, such as Germany and Japan before 1940, have tended to recover relatively quickly after defeat even though the physical base of the economy has been devastated.

2 Measuring what is produced

This section identifies the equality between income, output and expenditure in measuring national income. It asks students to identify the different elements of national income and shows the relationship with the circular flow of income. Aggregate demand is introduced and the implications of the equilibrium discussed.

❸❷❸ Activity: To compare size and growth of national income between countries

IT Students could interrogate the Nuffield Investigations and Data disk or the *Data Book* to see how national income has changed over time for different countries. They could be asked to rank countries in terms of the size of change of national income. Or they could be asked to project forward what the national income of these economies will be in 25 years' time.

The further research section suggests the use of the Eureco or World Trends Databases to explore components of national income. These can also be used to lay the foundations for the next section in which the sources of growth are explored.

3 The sources of growth

This section unites micro- and macroeconomics by showing how the growth of individual firms causes economic growth. This is related to shifts in aggregate demand and supply. The effects of government policy are also discussed.

An activity from Nuffield Investigations and Data, which asks students to compare a range of variables with growth, is suggested in the *Student's Book*.

❸❷❹ Investigation: Growth in the firm and the economy

To investigate the similarities and differences between the growth of a firm and the growth of an economy.

What makes a firm grow? This activity is intended to help the student to transfer understanding about growth in a firm to growth in the economy. It is important to bring out the idea that a growing firm will grow because it is increasing its use of factors of production. Different firms will grow in different ways, some remaining labour-intensive, others becoming capital-intensive. As with an economy, the firm has to make the best use of its factors of production.

Groups may select a firm making a specific product. They can identify the factors which would lead to growth of the firm. What would be the costs of such growth?

They then look at the economy and identify similarities and differences in the achievement of growth. Each group should present its findings about individual firms to the class, so that a composite picture will be developed.

AC ❸❷❺ Activity: The effect of technological change on the PPF

The photographs represent the changes that have taken place in the economy. Students are asked to explain the effect of such change on the economy as a whole and show that they understand the workings of a PPF.

They are then asked to consider how the PPF relates to the idea of aggregate supply, and it would be useful if they could explore the links between the two approaches. Questions 3 and 4 require students to consider the role of trade and of the structural changes which lead to people and other resources moving into new kinds of productive activity. They should be able to see the links between capital intensive production, economies of scale and international markets.

4 Malaysia: a newly emerging country

Malaysia is used as an example of a newly industrialising economy. The ideas introduced in the previous section are put to work in a new context. Direct foreign investment and the impact of multinationals are discussed as well as the problems which growth can bring to an individual country.

Questions 4b in the *Student's Book* should establish how students perceive economies at different stages of development. It is important for the teacher or lecturer to correct mistaken stereotypes. For instance, it is not true that most citizens of low-income countries are starving. Equally, it is very important to bring out the sophistication of parts of even some of the lowest-income countries' economies. Dual economies, where a Western-type economy runs parallel with a relatively backward economy, are the norm in Third World countries. Income distribution data could be used to reinforce this point.

AC ❸ ❷ ❻ **Activity: Still in the fast lane**

'Still in the fast lane' is a short article from the *Financial Times*. It can be used with material in this section to identify the problems associated with growth and identify a strategy for the future. The students' policy suggestions are unlikely to be sophisticated but they will lay foundations for later macroeconomic work.

5 Interpreting the data

Having gained an impression of growth in various countries, it is important that students realise that data can mislead. The section identifies the main methods of interpreting data of this kind. The activities, both here and in the *Student's Book*, are designed to reinforce that understanding. Questions 5a ask them to identify some of the issues and 5b is a simple exercise which is intended to help students to understand that the size of an economy and the standard of living of the citizens in that economy are not correlated. The standard of living is related to GDP per head.

IT Eureco or The World Economy data sets will provide material with which to carry out further comparisons. Eureco has an investigation entitled 'Growth and Living Standards' in the handbook.

AC ❸ ❷ ❼ **Activity: UK growth**

This activity gives some simple practice in dealing with index numbers. The answer to question 3 is that the data do not tell us anything about the size of any sector. Only changes can be deduced from the data given. The message, that overall growth rates conceal considerable variations between sectors and products, should be clear from this activity.

6 What are the costs and benefits of growth?

This section builds on material about externalities, which was covered in Stage 2. It looks at methods which are being developed and used to measure the effects of growth. Finally, it reminds students that growth has benefits which have led to an improvement in the standard of living for many of us.

AC ❸ ❷ ❽ **Activity: Growth and the environment**

This is a real example of the issues faced when decisions are made about expansion. It enables students to identify the external costs incurred when developments which would lead to economic growth are planned and to evaluate the costs of that growth. It could be used as role play, group work or as a case study for individual students.

❸❷❾ Activity: Counting the costs

National accounts only show total output, income and expenditure. If they are to represent the real impact of growth they must take environmental factors and reduction in welfare into account. This is easier in theory than in practice.

Students should work in groups to answer the following questions.

1 What factors should be taken into account when national income is reinterpreted to take account of the real costs of growth?
2 How can these factors be measured?
3 Can you identify any problems which may crop up in devising such a scheme?
4 On what conditions would this data be useful for international comparison?

Blueprint For A Green Economy by David Pearce, Anil Markandya and E.B. Barbier (Earthscan, 1989) would be useful background reading for this activity.

`AC`❸❷❿ Activity: Japan's miracle economy is bent on committing hara-kiri

This article takes a hard look at life in Japan and at the events after the boom years. Students should attempt to evaluate the impact of rapid growth.

❸❷⓫ Activity: The good old days

The objective is to identify perceptions of the changes that have taken place in the standard of living.

Students should ask their parents and grandparents to compare life now with life when they were 17. It would be helpful if the class could identify specific topics to ask about. They should note the year so that comparisons can be made.

A broader picture can be gained if students from a range of geographical backgrounds are in the class, as international comparisons can then be made. Differences in male/female perceptions of standards of living may emerge: this would add an extra dimension to the discussion.

7 What's happening to the UK?

❸❷⓬ Activity: What's happening to the UK?

This section provides an opportunity for students to start plotting events in the economy.

It could be done as a whole-class activity, where information is recorded on the charts on the wall. The Banking Information Service (10 Lombard Street, London EC3V 9AT. Tel. 0171-626 9386) has a wall chart for this purpose. As an individual activity, an annotated record would be a useful contribution to the portfolio.

This is an activity which is designed to give students a feel for the changing pattern of economic variables. Once recorded, they can be discussed and subsequently updated.

❸❷⓭ Activity: A debate

This activity uses the media material which students have been collecting while working on the unit.

Possible areas of focus for debate

➤ Should governments intervene to promote growth?
➤ Much more government intervention is needed to raise the standard of living.
➤ Government intervention hinders rather than promotes growth.
➤ Governments should keep growth rates at sustainable levels.

This debate should result in students using evidence and a limited range of economic theory. It is laying the foundations for later work on booms and slumps and on government influence on the economy.

8 Any lessons to learn?

This section draws the unit together and introduces the idea of sustainable economic growth.

③ ② ⑭ Activity: To build an image of the UK

At the beginning of the unit it was suggested that students should collect newspaper articles which discuss events in the economy, environmental damage which is occurring, benefits accruing to a country/firm or individual, or examples of how firms/economies are growing anywhere in the world.

Use these materials as the basis for group work in order to identify:

➤ Patterns of growth in the UK economy
➤ The costs of growth
➤ The benefits from growth
➤ How the situation in the UK might be improved.

Groups might give presentations or write up reports on different aspects of growth.

This would be a good basis for a portfolio contribution.

AC ③ ② ⑮ Activity: Investigating the impact of investment

This is an activity which asks students to calculate the effect of different levels of investment. It uses simple capital output ratios to explain growth differentials.

Stage 3: Unit 3 Why trade?

The unit focuses on

- Exports and imports
- Multinational enterprises
- The gains from trade
- Exchange rates
- Capital movements
- Import controls
- International institutions
- The balance of payments
- Elasticity of supply

Further ideas encountered

- The role of the EU
- The IMF
- GATT
- The European Exchange Rate Mechanism
- The elasticities approach to exchange rate changes

General advice

Although previous units have used case studies and examples from other countries, this unit is the first in which an entirely international context has been used.

From here onwards, students should be able to adopt an open economy perspective in all of their thinking. It is important that they consider trade as it affects all countries and not just the UK.

The unit also provides a good opportunity to study the European Union and its impact and to learn something about other international organisations.

A balanced consideration of trade requires that students be aware of trade in services as well as in goods. All these factors should be borne in mind when planning classroom activity.

Throughout the unit, students should use their prior knowledge, with particular reference to marketing issues, efficiency, price theory and structural change.

1 Why do firms export?

This section tries to impart something of the very diverse nature of UK export activity. It goes on to explore the benefits export markets can bring and the nature of competitiveness.

Questions 1b encourage students to make links with 'How do firms expand?' (S3/1), showing how the marketing strategies they have learnt about might be used in an international context.

AC ❸ ❸ ❶ Activity: Who exports? Why?

The activity pursues this theme and then asks students to think about and find out about local exporters. They should be encouraged to think about invisible exports as well as the visible ones. The activity can be kept short by splitting the class into groups, each pursuing one possible firm. It may be advisable to start this activity ahead of the unit, to allow time for gathering information.

2 Why do we import?

Attention now turns to the consumer, who can be seen to benefit directly from imports. By focusing upon footwear, it encourages the students to examine their own and their families' decisions.

The section helps to lay foundations for the study of comparative advantage in Section 4. Questions

2b invite students to draw conclusions about the effect of trade on real incomes.

The two activities below will not appeal to everyone, but are possibilities from which a choice can be made.

❸❸❷ Investigation: What are you wearing on your feet?

The task is to survey the family's footwear. The objective is to find out where the shoes were made and what determined the decision to buy them; the point is to explore the nature of competitiveness. The biggest problem will be that, with older shoes, it is harder to identify the origins. One possible way around this would be to return to the shop and ask.

Students should focus on a number of recently purchased pairs of shoes about which it is possible for them to find the necessary information. They should find out:
➤ Type of shoe
➤ Purchaser – could be themselves, a family member, or a friend
➤ Country of origin
➤ Reasons for choosing
➤ Selling points
➤ If imported, reasons why they did not buy a British product.

The conclusion: students could work in pairs to produce a short report on their findings, which should focus on the reasons why trade in footwear is important to consumers.

An alternative approach would be to investigate a shoe shop. If you have an independent shoe retailer locally, they may be able to tell you a great deal about trade in shoes. Important questions could cover the shop's buying strategies and the reasons for them, the proportions of imports and UK-produced shoes, and recent changes in these. Where is the competition coming from and why?

Retail chains tend to be less helpful than independent retailers.

❸❸❸ Activity: The footwear market

The objective here is simply to get the student to use the knowledge they already have of markets in general, in combination with their everyday understanding of a commonplace product.

Student task

Most of us know quite a lot about the market for shoes. The objective now is to analyse this with the aid of the ideas you have learned so far on this course. You need not step outside the classroom but think about all you have learned and how it can be made relevant to the market for shoes.

All these questions require a quite detailed answer.
➤ What determines the demand for shoes?
➤ Is the demand for shoes elastic?
➤ Is the demand for any particular type of shoe elastic?
➤ Is the market for shoes segmented?
➤ Is advertising a major factor in people's choice of shoes?
➤ What determines the supply of shoes?
➤ Under what circumstances might a shoe manufacturer find that profits and ROCE were falling?
➤ What strategy might the manufacturer adopt to deal with such a situation?

3 How do multinationals emerge?

Some work will already have been done on multinationals in the two previous units. This is an ideal time to look at the ethical questions raised by some multinational activities. The open questions at the end of the section may be helpful and a full-scale debate may be appropriate. The objective should be to have an adequate supply of newspaper/journal articles on a range of ethical issues, which can be drawn on for background.

4 Why do we trade?

A deliberately non-technical approach is used here, but the significance of opportunity cost should be emphasised in teaching. Students will not be expected to tackle numerical questions about comparative advantage in examinations but they should understand the nature of the theory and be able to follow the arguments.

The long case study on Chile could be used for more extensive questions than those asked in the text. If an activity on comparative advantage is thought desirable, this provides a wealth of material.

The subsection, 'Exploiting comparative advantage: the EU', looks at the fundamental rationale for its existence. This creates an important opportunity to develop understanding of its place in the UK economic situation.

It is important for students to understand the distinction between comparative and competitive advantage.

AC ❸ ❸ ❹ Activity: Investigating the impact of the EC on the UK economy

This requires students to consider some basic data for themselves.

5 Some problems with comparative advantage

It is not necessary to go through the traditional objections to the theory. However, the text states that 'the prices at which things are sold reflect their true costs of production'. You may wish to relate this to work done on externalities in Stage 2, showing how market imperfections may force us to reassess the gains from trade.

Here again the Open Questions should lead into some discussion of the ethical questions involved. It should be possible to identify recent examples of trade disputes involving the environment, which students can consider. Here again, it is

important to have a collection of fairly recent newspaper cuttings.

6 The importance of the exchange rate

Earlier work on competitiveness is built on here to develop understanding of the exchange rate. It is important that students get into the habit of translating a situation into a diagram and if the working questions are not used for this, some other strategy should be employed.

The working questions in this section will provide a lot of practice in analysing exchange rate changes.

Questions 6b deliberately force students to apply supply and demand analysis in the unfamiliar context of the exchange rate, without too many clues. The questions in both this and the next section tend to be difficult. There would be much to be said for their being done in the classroom where help is readily available.

Always in the short run, and sometimes over the longer run too, it is likely that capital movements will dwarf trading influences on the exchange rate. This may need some emphasis when teaching this topic.

7 Fixing, floating and the UK experience

This section was written with a 1993 perspective. It is to be hoped that students will see the issues in historical context. Alternatively, the approach can be adapted if the exchange rate regime has changed too much.

IT 'For further research' suggests using the Nuffield Investigations and Data disk to explore the relationships between the exchange rate, capital flows, exports and imports. Any other suitable database could be used for this. If Eureco is used, EU-wide comparisons are possible.

❸❸❺ Investigation: Influences on the exchange rate

Hypothesis
It is possible to trace the effects of inflation and interest rates on the UK exchange rate index.

IT If students are able to access data (preferably via IT but the *Data Book* will also give some) on DM, $ and sterling interest rates and inflation rates, they will be able to examine this question. They need to think first how sterling interest and inflation rates compared, before trying to link it to the exchange rate. The able ones may remember from earlier in the unit that there were other influences, such as North Sea Oil and the ERM.

AC ❸❸❻ Activity: Adjusting to exchange-rate changes
This activity is intended to test understanding of the whole area of exchange rates and might be appropriately used when students have reached the end of Section 7. The last two questions are intended to ensure that students consider current circumstances and evaluate the situation they observe.

The Open Questions near the end of the section highlight the need for keeping the analysis of exchange rates up to date.

happens when trade disrupts the structure of production. It is vitally important that some sense of balance is preserved here. In any trading situation, students should practise identifying gainers and losers and looking at their relative claims on government sympathy. This becomes important again in Section 10 on import controls.

❸❸❼ Activity: Gainers and losers in the footwear market
Figure 1 and Figure 12 in the *Student's Book* show that the UK market for footwear has grown. (Why is this?) At the same time, import penetration has increased. Identify the effect of each of these changes on the UK consumer, the UK worker in the footwear industry, the owner of, or shareholder in, the UK footwear producer, and the worker in, say, the Taiwanese footwear industry. How numerous are each of these groups?

AC ❸❸❽ Activity: Lotus Shoes
Here we have a firm which has survived in the face of strong competition. The objective here is to get students to relate that survival to what they learnt in Stage 2 about promoting efficiency. Trade can force firms to adopt strategies which cut both costs and, in relative terms, prices, so that consumers gain from increased competition as well as from the availability of imports. This is just one of the ways in which trade can promote efficiency. This is an ideal opportunity to integrate what students have learnt in different parts of the course.

8 Adjusting to change

The first subsection introduces elasticity of supply for the first time. This is done in a very specific context and it is important that students become able to transfer their knowledge of it to a completely different situation, e.g. the housing market. This should be tried out within a few weeks.

The second subsection looks in detail at what

9 Controlling the world economy

The purpose of this section is simply to ensure that students are not defeated by unfamiliar acronyms and are aware of the nature of the main international organisations. It could be used purely for reference or could provide the background for study of recent events involving international co-operation.

10 Should the government restrict imports?

Work on import controls provides an opportunity to apply basic price theory in a new context. Questions 10b deliberately avoid giving the tax incidence diagram, while giving a clue which may help the students to work it out for themselves. Still, these questions are difficult and help will probably be needed. It might be prudent to arrange for these questions to be done under supervision. The working questions in the *Student's Book* provide extensive practice in using the price theory underlying analysis of import controls.

In Questions 10b/2 and 3, it has been assumed that students will estimate a lower elasticity for trainers than for T-shirts, given the importance of branding in trainers. If they come up with similar elasticities, they won't arrive at a very interesting conclusion. If these questions are addressed in the classroom it will be possible to ensure that the conclusions are meaningful.

Here again, a bit of price theory is being explained for the first time in an international context and it is important to ensure that students can transfer the knowledge to other situations. It may be possible to review tax incidence a few weeks later in a different context, e.g. tobacco.

❸❸❾ Investigation and debate: Import controls are not an aid to employment creation

The whole issue of import controls can be debated by the class. It is important to ensure that participants use economic arguments and avoid emotive statements. Important links can be made to the whole question of equity and it may be possible to use some of the arguments developed in 3/3/7 'Gainers and losers in the footwear market'. This could be linked to an investigation of the expected effects of the Uruguay Round. There was good newspaper coverage of this in December 1993 following the conclusion of the negotiations, which should be accessible on CD-ROM. There are opportunities in this for weighing up the interests of consumers, producers and other stakeholders.

11 Should there be import controls?

Although there are no Open Questions here, there may be recent or current examples of trade which are ethically worrying to some people, yet still encouraged by GATT, or else of recent policy changes motivated by ethical considerations. These could be used as a basis for discussion or debate. The debate could be part of that suggested in 3/3/9.

AC ❸❸❿ Activity: Trade and the environment

This activity takes up the issue of GATT and the environment in more detail. The questions at the end could be a basis for role play or debate.

12 The balance of payments

It should be possible to use an updated version of Figure 16 to follow recent developments in the balance of payments. The importance of capital movements should also be emphasised.

Little is said here about government policy on the balance of payments. Questions 12d require students to explore the effect of trade imbalance on the exchange rate, and the effect of the resulting exchange rate changes on imports and exports. Given the earlier coverage of exchange rates, students should be able to work these out. Detailed consideration of the possibilities of macroeconomic policy must await 'What happens in booms and slumps?' (S4/1). It will be examined in more detail in Option 2, 'Can we control the economy?'.

AC ❸❸⓫ Activity: Some international trading stories

This activity outlines some more trade contexts for students to consider, drawing on various parts of the unit.

Stage 4: Unit 1 What happens in booms and slumps?

The unit focuses on

- The four stages of the business cycle
- The circular flow of income
- Injections and leakages
- The multiplier and the accelerator
- Unemployment
- Inflation
- The importance of money
- The effect of the cycle on people and business
- Confidence and expectations
- Macroeconomic policy

Further ideas encountered

- Cash flow and stock control
- Insolvency
- Income and price elasticity of demand
- Keynesian and monetarist policies
- International interdependence
- Moving averages

General advice

This unit develops the idea of cyclical changes in economic activity. It deliberately introduces a lot of quantitative data to allow the development of a degree of confidence in handling and interpreting it and an understanding of its role in business and economics.

How this unit is treated in teaching situations will depend partly upon the current state of the business cycle when the unit is being taught. Every effort should be made to relate the learning process to current events. At the same time, students must be aware that things could look very different in two or three years' time, and should also develop a feel for past phases of the cycle.

The questions in the *Student's Book* deliberately encourage students to keep revised, and to use, appropriate microeconomic and AS/AD diagrams, showing the links with previous work.

1 The effects of recession and slump

A good way to start work on this unit would be to use the student investigations on Laura Ashley, which are among the suggested activities for the Nuffield Investigations and Data disk. (It should be remembered that Laura Ashley had some other problems besides the recession.) This investigation opens up the whole question of how individual firms are affected by the business cycle, which can be explored in detail before going on to the macroeconomic angle.

In thinking about survival strategies, students should be encouraged to review all the potential cost–cutting/efficiency-increasing measures explored in Stage 2. (Activity 4/1/2 takes this up.)

It may be more appropriate to adapt Activity 4/1/1 to recovery or boom and use it with Section 2, if trading conditions are, once again, difficult by the time this unit is being taught. The point is to ensure that students are familiar with all stages of the business cycle.

Questions 1a and 1b aim to get students to see the relevance of income elasticity of demand to individual products' degree of vulnerability to the business cycle.

4 1 1 Activity: A local company in recession

Consider a company in your area, which survived the recession of the early 1990s. Ask the following questions, as well as any others you think important:

➤ What happened to the number of people working on the premises? Were there redundancies or natural wastage?

➤ Were any new buildings put up in the early 1990s?

➤ Were the staff on short time working at all?

➤ Were there large quantities of unsold products?

➤ What other strategies did the firm employ in order to survive?

AC ❹❶❷ Activity: A company which grew during recession

This is a case study of a company which saw the recession coming and reacted vigorously. It highlights the need to look at each business's experience as a totally individual one, nevertheless keeping trading conditions in mind.

2 The effects of recovery and boom

This section pursues the same approach for different phases of the cycle.

Questions 2a alert students to the link which can develop between income growth, consumption and the housing market.

❹❶❸ Investigation: The phases of the business cycle

Students can be divided into pairs or groups, each one taking one phase of the business cycle. The groups should first be encouraged to marshall all the relevant things they already know, both theoretical and applied. They should use AS/AD analysis to describe the phases of the cycle and show how the multiplier is relevant to an understanding of the changes which take place. They should then explore a database with the main economic indicators for the past 20 years. The database could be the Nuffield Investigations and Data disk economic background data, or Eureco, Economics of Europe Database, or this could be done

using the *Data Book* if the IT approach is impossible. Students should identify the occurrences of their phase of the cycle in the data on output, inflation, unemployment, investment, stockbuilding and so on. They may be able to investigate the time lags involved if they have access to the SECOS data-handling program. They should also consider the impact of the business cycle on individuals.

IT The Nuffield Investigations and Data disk has suggested investigations on the influences on consumption and investment in the section 'The Domestic Business Environment'. These can be pursued here or used in combination with 4/1/4, 'The business cycle since 1979'.

When their investigations are complete, each group should present its findings to the class. A composite picture of the whole cycle builds up, employing students' existing knowledge and drawing together all the groups' findings.

This investigation can take several hours but, if carefully done, can encompass all of the teaching needed to cover Sections 1–5 of this unit.

3 Trends and fluctuations

In examining the macroeconomic aspects of cyclical change, students should keep in mind the work done in 'What makes an economy grow?' (S3/2). This covers the long-term trend side of economic change, which acts as a backdrop to the short-term fluctuations. Students need to become fully aware of the difference between long-term trends and short-term fluctuations. They should appreciate that current changes will embody both to some degree.

The possibilities of investigating generally with the Nuffield Investigations and Data disk are mentioned in 'For further research' at the end of this section in the *Student's Book*.

❹❶❹ Activity: The business cycle since 1979

Students should make a chart showing the course of the UK business cycle since 1979. It should identify the time periods covered by each of the four stages of the cycle, pinpoint turning points in the growth of output, inflation and unemployment, and include election dates. Space should be left to add on significant details of government policy as they learn about them.

This can be undertaken at any time during work on this unit. (Or it could be combined with 4/1/3 'The phases of the business cycle'.) Data on output, inflation and unemployment can be drawn from any data source or from this section and Section 5 of the unit.

AC ❹❶❺ Activity: UK output and moving averages

'UK output' requires the student to graph the long-run trend output against actual output, and to work out how quickly the economy would need to grow after a period of stagnation in order to get back to that trend.

IT 'Moving averages' is a straightforward calculation. Both exercises can be done on spreadsheets.

4 What keeps the business cycle going?

This section turns in earnest to the economic theory underlying the business cycle. The multiplier and accelerator are deliberately dealt with in the simplest possible terms. Attention is drawn to the volatility of investment, compared to the relative stability of consumption. Students should understand the significance of this in creating the fluctuations of the business cycle. They will need to make connections to work done earlier on the phases of the business cycle, in order to see how these ideas explain the turning points of the cycle.

Students are encouraged to look at the circular flow of money from an open economy viewpoint, e.g. in Questions 4b and 4d.

AC ❹❶❻ Activity: Recession

This explores the effects of recession through the data for retail sales, industrial production, housing starts and first-time buyers' ability to buy.

5 Inflation and unemployment

This section simply explores both problems in more detail. Students should analyse events from 1993 to the present, creating an up-to-date analysis of events.

AC ❹❶❼ Activity: European comparisons

IT It may be useful at this point to review other EU countries' performance. Students should work in pairs or small groups. They should not confine themselves to the data provided but should use productivity data, inflation rates and so on to broaden the scope of the investigation. In seeking causal factors, data on education, earnings increase, etc., may prove useful and, finally, they should refer to factors not easily captured in the available data, e.g. immobilities. It may be possible to bring some data up to date with Eureco.

6 The business cycle and the government

This section highlights the controversial problems and invites students to develop their own views. It is used as an opportunity to introduce some very basic detail on the contribution of Keynes, placed in the context of his own lifetime. It is impossible to survey the 1980s without referring to monetarism and the Friedman viewpoint but, given the decline from prominence of these ideas in recent years, it seems wise to avoid too much detail.

AC ❹ ❶ ❽ Activity: The 1988 Budget

This uses the 1988 tax cuts simply as a comprehension exercise – a snapshot in time. Obviously, it is quite important to avoid giving the impression that the overheating was all the fault of the tax cuts, when there were so many complex causes, not least banking deregulation, the details of which are rather beyond the scope of this unit. Students may be able to identify the importance of the low level of savings for themselves, however.

7 What is the impact on individuals?

This section emphasises the effects of recession on the individual, although occasionally making the point that booms can have more attractive effects. If it is desirable to adopt an investigative approach to this question, then students can undertake a small survey of individuals.

8 Market forces at work

The objective here is to take what has been learnt in the middle sections of the unit and return to a consideration of the experiences of individual firms. Two case studies are given, which cover a long period and a number of phases of the business cycle.

AC ❹ ❶ ❾ Activity: The business cycle and different sectors

The general point, that some products are much more affected by the business cycle than others, has already been made. Students should make reference to income elasticities in their answers, also to the role of international competition in the case of clothing. This activity provides data which give some overview of both trends and fluctuations.

9 The international dimension

Students should now begin to integrate all that they have learnt so far. Motivation, profit, government policy, production efficiency, human resource management strategies, investment, growth and international trade are all elements in the questions they have to address.

At the end of the unit, students should be examining a problem which is currently newsworthy, involving business reaction to trading conditions, government macroeconomic policy and relations with other countries. The case studies given in the *Student's Book* represent relevant problems at the time; the choice of issue should reflect events when the time comes.

Stage 4: Unit 2 What is the impact of shock?

The unit focuses on

- The nature and cause of shock
- Import penetration
- Corporate culture
- Entrepreneurial ethos
- External and internal pressures
- Resistance to change
- Flexibility
- Regional multiplier
- Unemployed and under-utilised resources
- Regeneration
- Regional policy
- Skills mismatch
- Human capital
- Social overhead capital
- Diversification

Further ideas encountered

- Insolvency
- Externalities
- Quality assurance
- Minimum efficient scale
- Frictional and structural unemployment

General advice

The unit explores shock in a national, regional, company and individual context. It demonstrates the inevitable inter-relationships between these elements when a major shock occurs. The positive and negative impacts are discussed as well as ways in which problems can be overcome.

The response of the firm and the process of adaptation which results from shock are explained and will assist students in their understanding of the internal functioning and development of a company.

Regeneration is a major topic in the unit. It combines the role of government assistance with the effect on firms. The policy is evaluated in the light of the change of direction which has taken place.

Students should be encouraged to recognise shocks, both small and large and note the impact and outcomes. Such current application of the ideas in the unit would contribute effectively to their portfolio.

1 What is shock?

This brief introductory section sets the scene for the unit. The fall of the Berlin Wall is taken as a theme because it had impacts on individuals, firms and economies. Questions 1a are aimed at revising centrally planned and market economies as well as encouraging students to be aware of changes that have taken place in the recent past. They could form the introduction to the research-based Investigation 4/2/1.

AC ④②① Investigation: A post-communist economy

In the unit Germany is used as an example. Because of the support the German government has been prepared to give, it is somewhat exceptional. By following another east European economy, students would have a useful comparison.

They could be asked to investigate a country under various headings in order to give them some guidance. The use of a library which has newspapers on CD-ROM or a good supply of back numbers will be an asset. It will also assist the students' research skills.

2 The effect on firms

In this section the main theme is the idea that

shock leads to the need to take decisions; it raises questions about how the structure and systems within an organisation can cope. It is treated contextually and prepares the ground for the next section where the process of adaptation is looked at in more detail. Questions 2a are intended to direct students to speculate about the problems rather than to generate the 'perfect' answer.

AC ④ ❷ ❷ Activity: Cricket's calamity

This activity can be the basis for class work or individual work. It uses demand and supply to analyse the effect of a supply shock on price. It asks students to consider how a firm might respond to the shock and what the effect would be on the industry if no measures were taken.

3 How do firms adapt?

Ideas of corporate culture and the nature of an organisation are relatively new to A Level but are the common currency of industry. Here, the themes are picked up again following their introduction earlier. They are also developed further and built upon in 'Can we plan for the future?' (S4/3).

The objective is to identify characteristics of firms which help them to deal with shock. This may be the way in which they are prepared to adapt suddenly or the degree to which the management style means that some shocks turn into change.

AC ④ ❷ ❸ Activity/Investigation:
BICC Group Principles

The copymaster provides the mission statement and corporate culture documents for BICC.

Students should each be asked to contact a company and ask for similar information. This will provide a range of examples which can be compared. British Airways, ICI, Sainsbury's and IBM, for example, all have explicit statements. Body Shop has a different kind of statement.

When the students have acquired them, it is worth taking copies to add to the stock of resource materials.

They could be used in the following ways:

1 A comparison can be made to see how firms vary and to identify the factors which are important to different types of company.

2 The students can be confronted with a range of problems and then asked how different companies might respond based on the statements they have provided.

The problems will be most effective if they are of the moment but the following are general in nature and make a starting point:
➤ A new product which the company wants to develop and market has negative implications for the environment. What should the company do?
➤ The cheapest source of an important raw material is from a country where the workforce is paid subsistence wages. If the purchase goes ahead and the deal hits the headlines, there will be much bad publicity.
➤ The possibility of buying a company crops up. It would provide a considerable boost to profit if it were successful but the risks involved are greater and the speed of return slower than those normally accepted by the company.

A useful source might be *Understanding Organisations* by C. Handy (Penguin, 1985).

4 The wider scenario

In this short, contextual section, a brief view of the short-term impact of the fall of the Berlin Wall is provided. It demonstrates how the initial euphoria changed to gloom when the costs were counted both in the East and the West. It explains the effect of import penetration on the industry of eastern Germany and the costs incurred through extra government spending. It also looks at the impact on one British company which lost its main market as a result. The company is a real example but its name has been changed for marketing reasons.

As time passes, it will be worth looking to see if the gloom fades and growth and prosperity emerge.

IT In 'For further research' at the end of the section, students are referred to Eureco and World Trends which can be explored to show trends in growth and trade since the fall of the Berlin Wall.

Newspapers on CD-ROM will show further developments.

5 Disappearing demand: the regional impact

Swan Hunter is used as an example to identify the results of the closure of a major employer. The comments in the article about the effect on other businesses in Wallsend lead to an understanding of the idea of a regional multiplier. It asks students to identify the external impact of the closure of the company. These issues develop into a general discussion of wasted resources and externalities.

❹❷❹ Activity/Investigation: A visit

By visiting an area, a much clearer picture can be gained of the impact of shock. Assisted areas are now much more generally spread around the country and are therefore more accessible. The ideas of wasted resources and externalities can be understood much more fully through first-hand experience. A local company which has been affected, sought assistance, or started up in the area as a result of assistance, makes a profitable source of first-hand experience.

Careful preparation will involve priming the company on the type of information students will be looking for. The

case study on Hattersley and Davidson, in the *Student's Book*, will give guidance.

It is also useful to have a general overview of the area from people who are actually involved in the regeneration process.

The following addresses are contact points for DTI regional offices. They may prove helpful in providing an overview and identifying companies which have received assistance and may therefore be willing to receive a visit.

England

DTI North East, Stanegate House, 2 Groat Market, Newcastle upon Tyne, NE1 1YN. Tel: 0191-232 4722/ Fax: 0191-232 6742.

DTI North West, (Manchester), Sunley Tower, Piccadilly Place, Manchester M1 1BA. Tel: 0161-838 5000/Fax: 0161-228 3740

DTI North West (Liverpool) Graeme House, Derby Square, Liverpool L2 7UP. Tel: 0151-224 6300/ Fax: 0151-236 1140

DTI South West The Pithay, Bristol BS1 2PU. Tel: (0117) 927 2666/Fax: (0117) 929 9494

DTI Yorkshire and Humberside 25 Queen Street, Leeds LS1 2W. Tel: (0113) 233 8235/70/ Fax: (0113) 233 8301/2

DTI South East Bridge Place, 88–89 Eccleston Square, London SW1V 1PT. Tel: 0171-215 0888/0171-215 0557/ Fax: 0171-215 0875

DTI East Midlands Severns House, 20 Middle Pavement, Nottingham NG1 7DW. Tel: (0115) 950 6181/ Fax: (0115) 958 7074

DTI West Midlands 77 Paradise Circus, Queensway, Birmingham B1 2D. Tel: 0121-212 5000/ Fax: 0121-212 1010

Scotland

Scottish Office, Industry Department, Magnet House, 59 Waterloo Street, Glasgow G2 7BT. Tel: 0141-248 2855/Fax: 0141-242 5691

Wales

Welsh Office Industry Department, New Crown Building, Cathays Park, Cardiff CT1 2NQ.
Tel: S Wales (01222) 825111/N Wales (01492) 44261/ Fax: (01222) 823088

Other agencies which may be helpful are:

British Steel (Industry) Ltd, Bridge House, Bridge Street, Sheffield S3 8NS. Tel: (0114) 273 1612

British Coal Enterprises, Station Road, Carcroft, Doncaster, DN6 8DD. Tel: (01302) 727228

Enterprise Agencies and Development Corporations exist in many areas and can be found in the telephone directory.

Job Centres may also prove helpful.

6 Assistance for regeneration

Regional policy, as a solution to the problem, is discussed in this section. The development of regional policy and its shift of focus from automatic to selective is explained and evaluated. The contextual material at the beginning and end is case studies of Sheffield. The first looks at the decline of the steel industry and the establishment and work of the Development Corporation. The second is of an old, established firm which nearly came to grief in the 1980s but has survived and is now thriving, having received assistance from various organisations.

AC ❹ ❷ ❺ Activity: Museum of Scottish lead mining

Group work would be the most effective method for this activity. It could also be used on an individual basis.

The material comes from an actual application and gives an insight into the form of material that has to be submitted. It is, however, considerably abbreviated. This provides the opportunity to ask the students about other information they might like to have before making a decision.

Finding the location on a map might also help them in their decision making.

Questions to pose

1 On the basis of the information available would you give the museum the grant they are asking for? Explain your decision. Bear in mind whether the objectives are achievable and what the likely impact will be on the local economy?
2 What other information would help you to make a decision?
3 Are such grants purely a business proposition or do they have wider motives? What might these motives be?

7 Should there be regional policy?

The free market and the interventionist approaches are explained here. Evaluations, which are carried out by consultancy groups for the DTI, are used in evidence as to the effectiveness of current policies. The difficulties of evaluating regional policy are also mentioned. The section is rounded off with a short discussion of European policy. This is reinforced by Activity 4/2/6 which asks students to decide which areas of Europe are likely to need assistance, before presenting them with a map which outlines the regions.

AC ❹ ❷ ❻ Activity: Regional assistance in Europe

Introduce this activity with a discussion of the types of area which should be eligible for regional assistance.

Using an atlas and a blank outline map of Europe, ask

students to identify areas which are likely to be in need of regional assistance.

Once they have done this give them the photocopiable map of areas which receive help and ask them to compare this with their own efforts.

This activity helps to raise awareness of the nature of EU economies.

IT 'For further research' in the *Student's Book* suggests use of *Regional Trends and District Statistics* in order to explore unemployment on a regional and local basis.

8 Winners and losers

In this section a variety of short case studies is used to demonstrate winners and losers from situations of shock. They show how shock can affect individual firms as well as regions and countries. Students are asked to identify the sources of shock, the factors which have created winners and what losers might be able to do to survive.

Corby is used as an example of a loser which recovered. It uses the ideas which have been developed in the unit to demonstrate how government assistance and a careful strategy can overcome the problems. It also asks students to identify why Corby has been more successful than some peripheral locations.

AC 4 2 7 Activity: How to sell Hatfield?

The copymaster sheets which accompany this activity provide a range of information about the Hatfield area.

Students should be asked to devise a marketing campaign to attract industry into the town after the closure of British Aerospace's production plant.

They need to consider:
➤ The likely market
➤ The cost of land in the South East compared with other areas
➤ The availability of grants – or lack of them
➤ Appropriate strategies to attract new industry
➤ How best to reach potential newcomers.

Stage 4: Unit 3 Can we plan for the future?

The unit focuses on

- Aims and objectives
- Strategic planning
- Budgeting
- Business plans
- Project planning
- Risk management
- Economic planning
- Change management

Further ideas encountered

- Scenario planning
- Probability
- Mission statements
- Variances
- Management by exception
- Trend analysis
- Work scheduling

General advice

This unit explores the idea of planning in human affairs with particular reference to planning in business and in the economy. Starting with simple applications in everyday life, planning is revealed as a basic tool for both achievement and survival. The terminology of planning is examined in some detail which also provides a conceptual framework for understanding how formal planning is orchestrated. Strategic planning is covered fairly thoroughly, with a brief survey of current academic theory in the field. The section on operational planning includes basic budgeting and provides a link towards explaining the typical small business plan. The focus on risk and uncertainty is essentially qualitative but does include simple numerate work on time series analysis and probability.

The concluding sections deal with public and economic planning. It is important here that students gain some historical background. The ideal of planning has arguably been one of the great themes of the twentieth century and has both advanced and receded since the Second World War. The tension between planning and market forces is a difficult, but very revealing, idea. More speculatively, it seems that the trend is now away from the more formal and rigid plans of the past towards a culture of flexibility and rapid response. There is rich potential here for wider reading, personal investigation and class debate.

There has been an effort to avoid questions in the *Student's Book* that are vague or trite and, instead, to give useful experience in using specific techniques or to raise more open-ended issues.

1 The idea of planning

This section aims to analyse the nature and purpose of planning.

Preliminary thought about planning can usefully be based on the students' personal experience. Activity 4/3/1 explores their thinking about the short- and medium-term future. Some interesting conclusions can probably be drawn from their choice of A level subjects and, further back, from their selection of GCSE options in Year 9. The idea of 'insurance' and contingency plans is worth some discussion.

AC ④ ③ ① Activity: Planning for your future

This activity could start with discussion regarding the purpose of higher education. The rather utilitarian view of some students may be confirmed by the questions that follow but qualitative and educational considerations are also important! Chapter 12 in *Economics* by David Begg et al. (McGraw Hill, 3rd edn, 1991) has some excellent material.

2 Horizons

Many public companies offer some statement of aims and objectives (unfortunately the two terms are often used as synonyms). These are often printed in annual reports. More and more public organisations are also adopting formal aims and mission statements. These are often prominently displayed or are readily available on request.

❹❸❷ Activity: Personal missions

The students can be asked to make an *anonymous* statement of their own aims and objectives for the next one/two/five years and then to add a one-sentence, personal-mission statement. For those who are willing, these could be shuffled in a 'basket', redistributed and then read aloud or otherwise presented to the whole group for consideration. Anonymity will obviously be most easily achieved by the use of a word processor/printer.

The group may find it interesting to know that a survey of Harvard business graduates in the early 1980s included the question: 'Do you have a list of written goals?' After ten years the students who had answered 'yes' had a financial worth many times that of the 'no's and were found to be both happier and more satisfied with their lives ...

3 Strategic planning

This is a subject with a vast literature, much of which is rather inaccessible to A level students. However, the basic idea is fairly straightforward and is best explored in context. It is possible that the school or college has a strategic plan which is not confidential and which could be discussed. Annual reports tend to be rather glossy and artificially upbeat but they are still worth consulting. It may be appropriate to invite a manager from a local firm to talk retrospectively about a strategic plan and how far it was fulfilled. *Exploring Corporate Strategy* by Gerry Johnson and Kevan Scholes, (Prentice Hall, 3rd edn, 1993) offers an excellent study of the IKEA furniture chain in Chapter 1.

AC ❹❸❸ Activity: Running a restaurant

This is a simple case study which might be used at this stage as a down-to-earth look at the practical problems of planning.

4 Making detailed plans

Budgets need only be covered here at an elementary level but it is most valuable to link the work clearly with key accounting statements. Calculation techniques for cost and sales variances are not needed but the simple idea of percentage variances as an agenda for management action is important. Only an awareness of scheduling and operations research techniques is necessary, with no calculations.

A local firm may be willing to reveal an out-of-date budget and students could explore how it was actually used.

5 Small business planning

This is a subject that students usually find interesting and enjoyable. Many of them can offer some first-hand evidence from a family business or a part-time/Saturday job. This might be a good opportunity for a company visit or to invite a representative of a small business to outline their experiences. Forest Furniture provides a simplified framework which covers the basic ground.

❹❸❹ Investigation: A small business investigation

It would be invaluable if the students are able to gain first-hand insight as to how a small business plans for the future and monitors its progress. This investigation may be most suitable for students in pairs or operating alone. Clearly, some fairly personal co-operation is necessary from the proprietors or managers of the firms concerned. It is likely that they will be reluctant to reveal detailed financial data and some specimen figures or generalisations may be all that are possible in this respect. However, the aim is to research the nature of a real business plan, how it was compiled and how it is being implemented.

A good basis for the enquiry would be the sample business plan formats published by the clearing banks. These are available from the business sections of all major branches. Most of these include a blank pro-forma with useful subheadings and specific questions directed at the entrepreneur. (Midland's is particularly recommended.)

If time permits, the students could devise their own business plans representing a personal or group idea for a viable business. This might make a very worthwhile portfolio item. Again, the business departments at all the high street banks should be able to offer some help.

AC ④ ❸ ❺ Activity: Exmoor Hairdressing Supplies

This is a longer activity that would work best for small groups. It is a staged case study where most will be gained by allowing time for reflection on the first part before moving on to the second. The story is very largely true and should challenge all the assumptions of simplicity and neatness that can be conveyed by a plausible business plan. You may be interested to know that 'Mr Barlow' is now enjoying life again as a technician in the technology department of a nearby comprehensive school.

6 Planning for uncertainty

This is essentially a fascinating subject. The opening is intentionally qualitative as the theme is about far more than statistics. Equally, some simple statistical awareness is a vital asset for every student and this is a good place for its further development. The numerate element could easily be extended if desired, including elementary decision trees, although these are covered in Option 5 'How are decisions made?'

7 Public planning

This is a huge area for the application of planning principles. Its historical background is valuable general knowledge but also reveals the way in which ideas about planning have changed with time. The 'Planning in retreat?' theme could prompt an interesting debate that will inevitably be political.

There is a good chance that a local public sector organisation will be ready to explain its planning process. Local government officials in planning departments are often very ready to help and have useful leaflets and local case study material. Any local trading estate/business park might provide a particularly relevant example of the strategic planning process.

AC ④ ❸ ❻ Activity: Concorde: an Anglo-French dream?

The story of Concorde spans the period from the high-water mark of post-war planning to the much more market-led environment of the 1990s. It makes an interesting contrast with the case of the Channel Tunnel which received its go-ahead long after the era of lavish support for public projects had ended. The high-speed rail link from the tunnel to London is another example.

8 Forecasting economic change

A broad understanding of key trends and events since 1945 (and awareness of the 1930s depression) is essential to this section. This precedes consideration of the government's proper role in economic management and planning and returns to the course theme of markets and their use as a system of resource management.

Economic forecasting is quite a high profile activity and its failures have been the subject of much recent publicity. This raises interesting questions about the difficulties of forecasting and planning the behaviour of complex human systems.

❹❸❼ Activity: Personal economic forecasts

The basic idea is to give students a chance to make their own economic forecasts for the six months ahead. *The Guardian* has run a competition among readers to find the most accurate forecast on a given range of criteria. In rather the same way, the students can be given your own set of criteria and can enter their forecasts on a printed form or on disk. Possible candidates for inclusion would be growth in real GDP, the rate of inflation, the number of unemployed, the PSBR, the balance of payments, the base rate of interest, and the change in fixed capital investment. These can then be stored until the agreed period has expired. Probably the most convenient source of data for your purpose will be the *Monthly Digest of Statistics* (CSO), but the *Employment Gazette* and data published by the banks and press coverage are useful alternatives. A competitive element in the exercise is inevitable and some prize might be offered.

A variant on personal forecasts would be for the students to form forecasting groups and to produce collaborative judgements. It would be interesting (and perhaps amusing) to compare the students' accuracy with the results for various academic and commercial forecasts – and with the chancellor's Budget statement.

To produce their forecasts, students need access to library copies (or relevant photocopies) of the *Monthly Digest*, *Economic Trends* and other CSO publications. The annual *Economic Profile of Great Britain*, published by Lloyds Bank, is also recommended. The Nuffield Investigations and Data disk and the *Data Book* should also be very useful.

The students will obviously get most out of the exercise by following the forecasting debate in the media. Ideally, latest results for the chosen economic indicators could be displayed on the classroom walls or added to a class database.

AC ❹❸❽ Activity: The 1990 Budget forecast

This was an especially inaccurate Budget forecast, although John Major was in good company with his assumption that recovery would begin in 1991. All the actual data are readily available but the key results for this activity are:

Actual data for 1990–1991	
Growth in real GDP	– 2.48%
Rate of inflation	+ 5.9%
Manufacturing output	– 5.33%
Fixed capital investment	– 9.86%

Source: *Monthly Digest of Statistics*; *Blue Book* (CSO)

It might make good portfolio material for the students to carry out their own analysis of the forecasts for the current year (see Activity 4/3/7 above).

AC ❹❸❾ Activity: The power of the market

This is a classic statement of Friedman's belief in free markets. The students should be encouraged to respond critically but with serious regard for the logic and the evidence.

AC ❹❸❿ Activity: 'My biggest mistake'

This is from the *Independent on Sunday* series, and Robert Scholey combines a seminal story of British industrial experience with an unfashionable, but trenchant view of change management. Contrasts with Tom Peters' arguments would be very interesting.

Part 2 The option books

Approaching the options

Introduction

The intention of the Nuffield courses is that the options will be covered in a quite different way from the stages. It is assumed that, by this time, students will have learnt study skills and will be ready to take responsibility for their own learning strategies. They will have absorbed a great deal of the fundamental content of the subject. They will be ready to use what they know in a wider range of situations, applying concepts to unfamiliar scenarios. It is vitally important that teachers ensure that students do use the analytical tools that they have learnt to the full. They must employ the information in the enquiries, together with the theoretical tools and concepts they know, to create reasoned evaluations of the issues with which they are confronted.

For the most part, the option syllabuses develop and deepen students' existing knowledge. Relatively few new concepts are introduced. However, students are expected to achieve a much stronger understanding of the fundamentals than they could possibly do during the stages.

The suggestions for option study are very much less prescriptive than those for the stages. It is intended that both teachers and students will devise their own pathways through the subject matter. They may or may not choose to follow the suggested pathways for enquiry.

Planning option study

In all six option books many of the enquiries require the gathering of information. As teachers will be all too aware, this takes time. Therefore, there is a real need to plan ahead, for both teachers and students.

We recommend that teachers decide as soon as they can which options are going to be on offer. Once this is clear, they will be able to keep an eye open for useful material and build up a classroom library of newspaper and journal material, books and any other resources they come across.

Students can be introduced to the fields they are going to study for the options well before they finish work on the stages. They can then begin to consider what information they are likely to need and begin the process of gathering it. This is particularly important where information from firms is going to be required. It will be desirable for students to make a start on this process before the end of the first year of the course. The summer break will then give them some time for writing off where necessary and perhaps also for library searches. The objective should be for students to have completed any time-consuming processes by the time the autumn term begins.

The outcome – an overlap between the stages and the options – is educationally beneficial anyway because the options build upon work done in the stages. The two can, and should, reinforce each other.

Using the option books

Each option book opens with general advice. Students are then asked to consider five enquiries, each of which will absorb about two weeks' study time. The enquiries should be approached in an investigative frame of mind. Students should study the scope of the enquiry and the opening questions, perceiving in them a focus for wide-ranging exploration. The opening evidence provides viewpoints and case studies which will further define the scope of the enquiry. The text which follows should be seen as one of a range of sources which can be used during the enquiry.

A general pattern can be used to approach each enquiry.

➤ Decide what the main issues are.
➤ Identify the data required.
➤ Marshal the arguments which are relevant to the main issues.
➤ Evaluate the evidence.
➤ Draw conclusions, qualifying them as necessary.

The 'pathways for enquiry' offer a range of possibilities which you will want to choose from and adapt to fit the circumstances. Alternatively, you may prefer to use a different approach, devising your own schemes of work. In the long run, especially, it is to be hoped that you will develop and refine the ways in which you advise students. There will be times when they need to be given guidance, and times when they can see a clear structure for their enquiry for themselves. Whenever possible, students should devise their own approaches.

Where individual students work in groups on different pathways, they can extend their knowledge and understanding by presenting their findings to the whole class.

In the sections which follow on each option, some 'useful resources' are given but there will be many more which both students and teachers will find for themselves.

Option 1: Poverty and Wealth: Is inequality inevitable?

This option is composed of five enquiries which investigate the subject in an integrated manner. As inequality is present in all parts of the world, each enquiry takes a global perspective and incorporates material from both the developed and the developing world to provide a backdrop for the application of economic principles.

The enquiries explore the various strategies which have been identified as methods of reducing inequality. The purpose is to evaluate their strengths, weaknesses and outcomes in order to decide on effective solutions to problems. The recognition that a complete solution is probably unachievable is also important.

It must also be borne in mind that solutions have their costs. When a change improves the lot of some people, who else will be affected? Trade-offs are a significant part of the debate, particularly in the last enquiry.

Poverty and Wealth builds on the work of the stages – What is efficiency?, Do markets work?, What makes an economy grow? and Why trade? are sources of important prior knowledge and should be revised.

Teaching this option

This option requires students to be aware of the issues which are current in the debate on inequality. The most effective way of raising awareness is to collect newspaper articles so that a store of information develops. Students should be asked to participate in this activity.

Newspaper articles from CD-ROM allow ready access to reasonably recent material. The identification of keywords which will produce appropriate articles is a skill which students need

to develop in order to demonstrate clear thinking about the issues involved.

Several of the books which have been recommended for pathways for enquiry look at issues from a particular perspective. Students need to bear this in mind when using them because it is important to realise that there is also an alternative view.

Several books are useful for all the enquiries in this option. They are mainly annual publications which are available from large public libraries.

➤ *The World Development Report* (World Bank, OUP)
➤ *The Human Development Report* (UNDP, OUP)
➤ *Social Trends* (HMSO)

Two of these are available on SECOS:
➤ *World Trends* on SECOS (World Development Report)
➤ *Social Trends* on SECOS

These and Nuffield Investigations and Data on SECOS are available from Statistics for Education, 5 Bridge Street, Bishops Stortford, Herts CM23 2JU.

Enquiry 1: How unequal is the world?

Synopsis

The opening evidence provides a range of material which explores both national and international dimensions of inequality. It uses different interpretations of poverty to show how people can fall out of society because of their lack of a variety of resources. The implications of inequality and the role of government are also raised.

1 What does inequality really mean?

The enquiry opens the discussion by identifying the important distinction between absolute and relative poverty, as shown by two case studies of poverty in the UK and Brazil.

2 Interpreting inequality

The data are then looked at more carefully, using purchasing power parities to enable students to realise that the values must be interpreted in the light of their spending power in each country.

3 The changing pattern

The changes that have taken place in the distribution of income, economic activity and standard of living are explored. Gini co-efficients and Lorenz curves are used in order to assist students to understand the differences more fully. These skills will be applied later in the option.

4 The causes of inequality between nations

This section of the enquiry lays the foundations for the option by looking at the causes of inequalities between nations. The role of the level of development itself, investment, the labour market and trade are introduced with reference to differences between nations.

5 The causes of inequality between individuals

Wealth, supply and demand, qualifications and discrimination are used to explain interpersonal differentials.

Pathways for enquiry

Rich world, poor world

In sections 2 and 3, the various methods of interpreting inequality are discussed. These, together with data which show standards of living in terms of consumer durables, education, health care, etc. can be used to produce a broader picture of the way of life of people in countries at different stages of development.

The World Trends Database on SECOS provides a wide range of data and the investigations in Study 1: Rich world, poor world develop this theme very effectively.

Identifying the causes of international inequality

The issues in Section 4 are an introduction to following enquiries so a general identification of factors which have made a specific country in each category of development more or less equal would lay the groundwork for future investigation. The level of development itself, investment, the labour market and trade, together with geographical factors of location and natural resources, will all assist in explaining the current state of affairs in a selected country. Not all information will be readily available but some conclusions should be possible on the basis of a selection.

What makes individuals unequal?

There is a considerable amount of data in the text which highlights differences. Much of it comes from the *Employment Gazette* and *Social Trends*. The latter is available as a data set on SECOS and relationships can be demonstrated by using tables together. Appropriate investigations can be identified from the guide which accompanies the disk.

Discrimination

Discrimination takes many forms but usually has the effect of reducing an individual's competitiveness in the market place. It is obviously a sensitive issue but its range and scope can be identified from newspaper articles. CD-ROM will therefore prove to be most useful as a source of material.

Useful sources

The resources recommended for the option as a whole are all useful for these enquiries.

➤ *Employment Gazette*, Department of Employment (often in public libraries).
➤ For information about specific countries, the following is useful: Geofile, available from Stanley Thornes, Ellenborough House, Wellington Street, Cheltenham GL50 1YD, Tel: (01242) 224234.

Enquiry 2: Can aid reduce inequality?

Synopsis

The opening evidence gives some examples of the type of work that is carried out through the provision of aid, the amounts of money that are given to different countries and the nature of the aid.

It also includes some issues that arise about the use and allocation of aid. Whether it goes to those who really need it is questioned in relation to arms spending. A cartoon asks whether the dependency that can result from aid is beneficial.

1 What is aid?

This section explains the different types of aid and how they are used. Bilateral aid is distinguished from multilateral aid, and concessional from non–concessional loans.

2 Giving and receiving

Donors and recipients are discussed, both in terms of who they are and why they give and receive. The political and economic motivations of both sides are introduced.

3 Can aid narrow the gap?

The effectiveness of aid in narrowing the gap between rich and poor is looked at in terms of the problems and benefits which may arise. The dual economy which can be created as a result of aid is raised as an issue. The development of an entrepreneurial culture may not occur if countries become dependent on aid. Its efficient allocation and the debate about whether it reaches its intended destination are both posed as problems.

Debt is discussed briefly but is looked at more thoroughly in Enquiry 4.

4 Development or dependency?

Dependency may lead to industrialisation being imposed on a country and the application of inappropriate techniques which may lead to rapid development in some sectors and little in others. The use of appropriate technology is discussed as a way of enabling gradual development to take place within a country's limitations.

5 Can aid be more effective?

The UN objectives for aid are calculated on the basis of 0.7% of GNP multiplied by one plus the difference between the donor's GNP per capita and the average of all donors. The actual quantity of aid given is compared with the much higher levels which the UN would like to see.

Pathways for enquiry

A recipient study

A recipient country might be studied in order to find the answers to the initial questions in the enquiry. By following the sequence of these questions, a picture could be built of the purpose, effects and side effects of aid. Oxfam is a useful source of information as it has people working on its behalf in many countries and therefore has first-hand information. It also publishes short books about specific countries, such as *Burkina Faso: New Life In The Sahel*, which provide details of the problems and of how aid is being used effectively or ineffectively.

A country which is highlighted in the press because of an aid issue might also provide the focus for such an enquiry. Does this country need aid more or less than others? Are there any strings attached? How is the money being used?

➤ Oxfam, 274 Banbury Road, Oxford OX2 7DZ.

A donor study

An investigation of the UK's (or any other country's) policy and practice in giving aid. Through this, students could follow up the countries to which aid is given and seek the justification and purpose of the donation. The EU is also interesting because aid is given multilaterally to assist in a variety of development projects as well as on an emergency basis.

Information about UK aid is available from The Overseas Development Administration, 94 Victoria St, London SW1E 5JL.

EU information comes from The Commission of The European Communities, 8 Storeys Gate, London SW1, Tel: 0171-973 1992.

Need or efficiency?

There are, undoubtedly, occasions when aid has to be given as quickly as possible in order to relieve hardship. On other occasions, should the efficiency of an aid package be subjected to as close a scrutiny as a business investment decision? By identifying a case study or an example from the press, some broad conclusions might be drawn about a particular donation, as to its costs and benefits. This may give rise to questions about appropriate technology and the best strategies for mobilising the workforce and other resources effectively.

How much more should we give?

Take the percentage of GNP which the UN would like to see from donors and work out what this is in terms of current spending. Identify what this amount of money would buy in terms of government spending. This provides a clear idea of the trade-offs that are involved in the debate.

Useful sources

➤ *The Greening of Aid*, ed. by Czech Conroy and Miles Litvinoff (Earthscan, 1988)

Enquiry 3: Can trade reduce inequality?

Synopsis

The opening evidence displays a range of examples of successful and unsuccessful effects of trade. The Asian tigers have reaped substantial rewards from trade but in other circumstances the outcomes may not be as beneficial.

Where a nation as a whole may gain from free trade and, therefore, in the long run, gains accrue to the population as a whole, some people will find that they are losers. Traidcraft shows how, on a small scale, some of these losers can become winners.

1 To trade or not to trade?

The first section raises the question of whether trade or protectionism is an effective way of dealing with inequality. The French music and film industries are cited as examples of how protectionism can allow a country's culture to continue to develop.

Export promotion and import substitution are identified as alternative strategies for development.

2 Export promotion: a source of growth?

The costs and benefits are explored of the export promotion strategy which has been used successfully by several fast growing economies. It must, of course, be remembered that these countries have not accepted free trade but have controlled imports severely in order to let their home markets develop. Another export promoter, Tunisia, demonstrates the importance of education and training in the process of becoming outward looking. Because growth is generally much faster for countries which take this route, the environmental impact may also be greater.

Export growth may come from primary products or a mix, including manufactures. There is also scope for increased trade between developing countries rather than just in the traditional pattern from developing to developed and vice versa.

3 An inward approach to success?

Import substitution is generally thought to be a slower method of development but some would argue that it protects the indigenous economic environment and structure of society. The process is demonstrated by a case study of the computer industry in Brazil, which was heavily protected in order to become established. Once opened up to trade, its future is less secure.

4 The impact of trading blocs and agreements

The roles of GATT, the EU and the North American Free Trade Area are discussed. The resulting changes in the pattern of trade and the impact on the developing world are investigated.

The effect of reducing tariffs in the most recent GATT round is investigated.

The continued links which the countries of the EU have with their ex-colonies have led to distortions in the market for certain primary products. The effect of the Lomé convention on the market for bananas is used to demonstrate this.

NAFTA has raised issues in both America and Mexico which show how the laws of comparative advantage may affect those involved in the opening up of trade.

5 Can the playing field ever be level?

International trade does not take place on a level playing-field. Child labour and appalling working conditions reduce costs in some countries, which scares producers in the developed world as trade becomes freer. NAFTA, for example, is trying to take account of these differences to some extent.

6 Does trade lead to equality?

The final section looks at whether trade has increased equality. The data suggest that, in the initial stages, inequality may grow but it is reduced in time. However, urban poverty in the developing world is growing as more people are drawn to towns and cities.

Pathways for enquiry

A data search

By gathering data on trade, growth and other indicators of an improving standard of living, students can identify patterns that exist and changes that are taking place in these relationships. World Trends on SECOS would be a useful source of data.

A country study

One of the Asian tigers would provide a good subject for study as much has been written about them from both positive and negative points of view. It is important to identify the standpoint of the author of many books in this field because much of the material is open to interpretation. An investigation of the growth pattern, education system, standard of health care, etc., in relation to their pattern of trading development, will provide a sense of how these factors move together. *The Economist* is a good source of short articles about these countries.

If students select a variety of countries, comparisons can be made. An import substitutor would be useful for comparison but information would be harder to collect.

Perspectives on free trade

GATT has reduced trade barriers significantly and this has affected EU tariffs. The effects of this are long lasting and commentators will be watching as various stages of the agreement are put into practice. A survey of the initial response to these changes and identification of outcomes will show how freeing trade can affect economies. Does it create more or less equality?

A level playing-field

The open market relies on competition. Some countries have competitive advantage in some areas of trade but others gain because externalities do not have to be accounted for and lack of legislation to protect both workforce and adjacent population means that costs are lower. Many companies and workers in the developed world feel aggrieved because they lose trade and employment to such countries. There are some examples in the text and students might identify others, evaluate the effects both locally and overseas and suggest solutions.

These issues generally reach public awareness when highlighted in the press. The information presented usually gives only one side of the argument. By using such an example, students could be asked to work out the other side of the story and draw some conclusions about the implications of the problem.

Alternative trading organisations

Traidcraft is the most famous example of an alternative trading organisation and is cited in the text. Students can use it as an example to identify ways in which small-scale enterprises might assist in other areas. They would first need to identify the range of Traidcraft's work or that of a similar organisation in order to suggest how assistance might be given to others who find themselves in conditions of hardship.

➤ Traidcraft Exchange, Kingsway, Gateshead NE11 0NE. Tel: 0191-491 0591
➤ Oxfam, 274 Banbury Road, Oxford OX2 7DZ

Useful sources

The following books all contain useful information about the range of issues which have been dealt with in the enquiry. The first two provide general background information, although the second has much exemplar material. The second pair are largely case study books and should be drawn on for specific country examples. The best way to find relevant information is through the index.

➤ *The Economist* has frequent short articles about trade-related issues.
➤ *Economics for A Developing World*, by Michael P. Todaro (Longman, 1992)
➤ *Industrialisation and Development*, ed. by Tom Hewitt, Hazell Johnson, Dave Wield (OU and OUP, 1992)
➤ *The Trade Trap*, by Belinda Coote (Oxfam, 1992)
➤ *Dragons in Distress*, by Walden Bello and Stephanie Rosenfeld (Penguin Books, 1992)

Enquiry 4: Is growth the solution?

Synopsis

The opening evidence demonstrates differing outcomes of growth or its absence and attempts to identify some sources of problems. It includes property rights, hunger, lack of education and debt as issues which may prevent growth. Providing that everyone is involved in the process, growth is advocated as a bringer of equality. However, rising unemployment is also a product of growth because, as industry throughout the world becomes increasingly capital-intensive, people may be made redundant.

1 Growth and the individual

In the first section correlations are made between growing GDP and spending on public health and life expectancy. The changing pattern in the second half of the century is also shown. India, Brazil and South Korea are used as contrasting economies. In general, as countries become more developed, they become more equal but the range within which this change takes place is very wide.

2 The labour issue

Increasing productivity has been outstripping the growth in employment throughout the world. Highly capital-intensive investment may reduce the demand for labour. The labour market is explored to identify ways in which people can become more effective participants in the economy. Land reform, entrepreneurship and the nature of government are all looked at as possible ways of giving people more involvement.

3 The transnational corporation: a spur to growth?

The role of transnationals is discussed to identify the benefits that they bring and also their drawbacks. There is case study material on a project that was initiated by a Unilever company in India, the problems stemming from the demand for cheap labour in Singapore and the power wielded by transnationals in Indonesia.

4 The debt trap

In attempting to grow, many countries, particularly in sub-Saharan Africa, have borrowed beyond their means. Debts can be substantially greater than GNP. This section explores how the crisis came about and the effects that it has had on the inhabitants of the countries involved. The various proposals that have been suggested are evaluated.

5 Growth and inequality

Growth differentials between countries are evaluated and trends explained. The effects of growth on individuals are looked at in terms of theory and practice.

Finally, the question is posed, whether growth brings greater equality, or greater equality creates an environment in which growth can take place.

Pathways for enquiry

Equality or inequality?
In some ways life becomes more equal as countries grow wealthy. Does it also become more unequal? Are there groups of people in either the developed or developing world who gain little, if at all, as economic growth progresses? Why does this happen? Are there any solutions?

Report from the Frontier by Julian Burger (Zed Books, 1987) provides case study material on the state of the world's indigenous peoples. It shows how development has not only passed them by but has actively made their lives worse.

The media often deal with such issues and television programmes or newspaper articles may provide a good stimulus. Remember that you will often see one side of the problem and the other must be identified as well.

What about the jobs?
Often growth has not led to proportionate increases in employment. Developing countries have increasingly installed hi-tech equipment which employs few and may require skilled staff from overseas. What can be done to make growth 'appropriate'? Are such solutions merely holding countries more firmly in the grip of underdevelopment or do they permit advancement to take place at a speed which does not destroy existing structures? Are existing structures worth preserving?

Japan rejected the 'appropriate' notion when the Americans suggested it! Look where they are today.

There are some very emotive questions in this pathway but they provide a challenge to explore.

It can incorporate the World Bank views of restructuring economies and the criticisms of the strategy that have been expressed.

It can also look at the role of transnationals and the impact they have on the local community.

Transnationals: always the sinner?
Transnationals receive a lot of criticism. Is it always justified? In order to come to a conclusion, it will be necessary to ask one what it does and why it does it. It would also be interesting to find out the views of the host country and a variety of commentators in order to be able to interpret a range of comments.

➤ *Applied Economics*, by Alan Griffiths and Stuart Wall (Longman, 4th edn, 1993) contains a useful chapter on transnational enterprise.
➤ Transnational companies such as Unilever or BP will generally supply information about their activities.

What about the debt?
In order to gain some understanding of the size of the debt problem, imagine that it was a UK problem. Calculate the likely repayments each year if our debt was equivalent to GNP. What effect would this have on government spending? Look at how spending is allocated and identify the proportion of cuts that would be necessary. This pathway makes a useful introduction for the next one.

Why not just cancel the debt?
Take the roles of a minister of finance from the debtor country, an education or health minister from a debtor government, a bank seeking repayment, a representative of the World Bank or other organisation which is attempting to find a solution. By looking at the problem from a range of perspectives, students will gain a greater understanding of the complexities of the issue.

➤ *The Philippines: Debt and Poverty*, by Rosalinda Pineda-Ofreneo (Oxfam, 1991)

➤ *Human Development Report* 1992, pages 45–7

➤ *How the Other Half Dies*, by Susan George (Penguin, 1986)

Enquiry 5: Do solutions have their costs?

Synopsis

The opening evidence contains a selection of views and issues concerning the effects of inequality and the costs of overcoming it. Korea, for example, has a better standard of education and health care than many equivalent countries but still has a repressive government which decides what can be printed in the papers. Editors are sent to prison if they contradict rulings. In the US, everyone is entitled to free education until they are 18 but in some parts of the country many never last the course and a high proportion are likely to be in prison. Another piece questions the value of the welfare state – does it make us too dependent? On a larger scale, the question is posed whether using the same solutions to the problems of the developing world, as are used in the developed world, will have successful outcomes.

1 Why do we seek equality?

The trade-off between inequality and efficiency is raise in the first section. Alternative interpretations of equity are also introduced. Marginal social costs and benefits are used as a yard stick and the problems of their calculation are introduced. The effects of inequality on the macroeconomy are also looked at.

2 Inside inequality

Sources of inequality which arise for reasons other than income are then investigated. The outcomes of health care systems which do not provide easy access for all are investigated. The holes in the net of the US private insurance schemes are used as a case study.

On the education front, the relationship between the level received and wages in different countries and occupations are explored The effects of education on infant mortality and fertility rates have implications for development plans in poor countries.

3 Achieving equality: in a national context

Ghana's strategy for development is used to introduce this section. Many items in the plan are familiar from the developed world. It aims to make the country more affluent but does not discuss ways in which greater equality can be achieved. The rest of this section looks at various ways in which governments might redistribute income, such as taxation, benefits and incentives which are aimed at making the market work more efficiently. The problems of growing demands on the welfare state are raised and some alternative pathways to dealing with the problem are introduced.

A brief mention of regional inequalities leads into the next section.

4 Achieving equality: in a European context

Some European comparisons are made here. Which areas are poorest and which receive assistance from the EU, and the nature of this assistance, are looked at.

5 Achieving equality: in a global context

This final brief section looks at the outcomes of existing patterns and identifies some problems which may arise in future. The issue of trade-offs is present as always. By creating winners in the growth stakes do we also create losers?

Pathways for enquiry

Inequality in the UK

To encompass the issues arising from inequality, and attempts to reduce it, a study of the UK economy would provide an overview of the issues. Students should start by identifying the degree of inequality in the country. This might be looked at from a consideration of income statistics as well as health, education, housing, crime, etc. in order to create a fuller picture.

A survey of the attempted solutions and their outcomes, with costs if they are available, would provide an insight into the effectiveness of government policy. A range of alternative strategies which are proposed by the opposition party or pressure groups could be evaluated to determine whether they would be more successful. Students should identify the trade-offs which would be necessary in order to carry out these policies.

The important question to be addressed is whether the costs of the policies outweigh the benefits.

The investigations involved in this pathway could be carried out in groups and pooled at the end to give everyone a broad picture.

This pathway will require the data sources which have been mentioned in the introduction to the option as well as reference to newspapers. Party election manifestos are useful, although it must be remembered that promises do not always turn into fact.

Inequality in the developing world

The same enquiry could be carried out for economies in the developing world. The data would be harder to come by and might have to be used on a more general regional basis. In the *World Development Report 1993*, the World Bank has produced some interesting data on the costs and benefits of improving health care in the developing world. Education is also recorded because there is a strong correlation between its availability, especially to women, and the take up of health care.

Select a country which has plenty of data available in the source books. Embassies may also be able to help. Addresses are listed in London *phone books*, which are usually available in libraries or main post offices.

Can the welfare state survive?

The provision of health care and education has played a key role in increasing equality. Both are now regarded as under threat. Both are services which rely heavily on people and therefore it is difficult to increase productivity. Other industries cut costs by replacing people with increasingly capital-intensive equipment, but this is not

an option which can make a significant difference to health and education. Health is also challenged by the changing age structure of the population.

How can scarce resources be allocated effectively in these circumstances? Students should raise questions of efficiency, equity, trade-offs and value judgements in looking at the issues involved. Data are available from the Department of Health, the Department for Education and local health and education authorities. The possible policy options, which are set out in Figure 5.13, give a guide to the range of alternatives.

➤ Department of Health, Richmond House, 79 Whitehall, London. Tel: 0171-210 5983
➤ Department for Education, Sanctuary Buildings, Great Smith St., London SW1P 3BT. Tel: 0171-925 5000

How important is the political complexion of the government?

In some of the countries which have been used as examples in the text, inequality has been reduced steadily, in others there has been little change. Is there a relationship between the nature of government and the pattern of inequality? By selecting a small range of countries, some comparisons could be made.

➤ *Development Policy and Public Action*, ed. by Mark Wuyts, Maureen Mackintosh, Tom Hewitt (OU/OUP, 1992) has several case studies on the role of government and the effect on development.
➤ A CD-ROM search may also produce articles about specific countries with information of use in the investigation.

Useful sources

➤ *Paying For Inequality* by Andrew Glynn and David Milliband (IPPR/Rivers, Oram Press, 1994)
➤ *Investigating Social Issues* by Jenny Wales, (Macmillan, 1990)
➤ *Welfare State Economics* by David Whynes (Heinemann, 1992)

Option 2: Government Objectives: Can we control the economy?

In considering how the economy may be controlled, the first approach is likely to concern the macroeconomic tools – fiscal, monetary and exchange rate policies. Operating directly on the level of aggregate demand, these are a vital component part of any government's strategy.

Over the course of the past two decades, realisation has grown that the macroeconomy is intimately linked to the microeconomy. To consider the possibilities of macroeconomic policy without taking the micro framework into account is to form an extremely partial view. The major macroeconomic problems have their roots, in part, in the individual actions of all decision takers in the microeconomy. In particular, inflation, unemployment and the policies needed to deal with them, require, if they are to be understood, some knowledge of how the labour market functions.

This is not easy for A level students to handle. It implies that they will have to draw together what they have learned in a number of different areas of the subject. Realistic analysis will rest upon wide-ranging knowledge and a competent grasp of the fundamentals.

However, they will already have studied price theory and business cycles in Stages 1 and 4, respectively, and the growth process and international trade in Stage 3. It is to be hoped that, while studying this option, they develop the satisfying feeling of watching all these strands come together and begin to understand some quite difficult issues.

Teaching this option

In a number of places the pathways for enquiry overlap. As choices will be made about which ones to follow, this does not matter. You may choose to combine two anyways, or split the class into groups who follow different pathways.

Throughout the option, one of the main tasks facing the student will be identifying the information that is required in order to shed light on the question in hand.

Probably the most extensive databases will be found to be the Economic Background data on the Nuffield Investigations and Data disk, together with Eureco, the Economics of Europe database and World Economic Trends (all available from Statistics for Education). If it is possible to use only one, then Eureco will give the best coverage. The Nuffield Project *Data Book* offers a hard copy alternative. The latest copies of HMSO's *Economic Trends* and *Blue Book* would be additional assets.

A number of free items are available:
➤ 'Economic briefings' from the Treasury, write to Economic Briefing (Distribution), Central Office of Information, Hercules Road, London SE1 7DU
➤ Fact sheets and 'bank briefings' from the Bank of England (Information Division, Bank of England, Threadneedle Street, London EC2R 8AH
➤ 'European Economic Perspectives', the newsletter of the Centre for Economic Policy Research, 25–28 Old Burlington Street, London W1X 1LB

Obviously, it is essential for students to keep up to date with current policy while studying these issues. Even if it is not possible to acquire a good daily paper, Sunday papers and/or *The Economist* all year round, then simply for the duration of this option, all possible effort should be made to do so. A number of sources will be found useful throughout the option:

➤ *An Introduction to the UK Economy*, by Colin Harbury and Richard G. Lipsey (Blackwell, 4th edn, 1993), provides comprehensive information on the UK economy. It goes considerably further than students will be required to do for this option but will be found useful for reference.

➤ A really detailed source for reference is *Applied Economics* by Alan Griffiths and Stuart Wall (Longman, 5th edn, 1993).

➤ The Heinemann series, *Studies in the UK Economy* has a number of useful titles. *The UK Economy* by the National Institute of Economic and Social Research (2nd edn, 1993) provides good general background.

➤ The Economist schools briefs, *Labour Market Economics*, appeared in 1994 and are available from Linda Denli, The Economist, 25 St James's Street, London SW1A 1HG. They cover many aspects of the labour market which are relevant to this option.

➤ *Britain's Economic Miracle*, ed. by Nigel Healey (Routledge, 1993), attempts to assess the progress made during the rule of Conservative governments from 1979 onwards. Each chapter addresses a particular issue.

➤ *The Economy Under Mrs Thatcher, 1979–1990* by Christopher Johnson (Penguin, 1991) goes into considerable detail and would be a little difficult for most students but offers a very thought-provoking view.

➤ It is worth considering using the simulation, *Running the British Economy*. This is a complex decision-making exercise incorporating all the main macroeconomic variables. It is available at £100 from The Esmee Fairbairn Research Centre, Heriot-Watt University, Riccarton, Edinburgh EH14 4AS. Although expensive, it can have a motivating effect on students.

Enquiry 1: What has been achieved?

This opening enquiry draws together and reviews the evidence on economic performance, primarily for the UK but with some references to other countries where comparison may be appropriate. From the student's point of view, the objective is simply to become better acquainted with the way the economy has developed in recent years. Familiarity with the data can be used as a sound basis for the study of a variety of policies in the remaining chapters. Thus the enquiry should lead the student to apply the theory they already know as they develop a much more sophisticated knowledge of recent events.

Synopsis

1 Objectives
The main aspects of government objectives are outlined: growth, low inflation, low unemployment and the balance of payments.

2 Trends, fluctuations and changing circumstances
This section highlights the difference between short-term fluctuations and long-term trends. It relates these to AS/AD analysis, which can be used to show both kinds of changes. It emphasises the difficulty of distinguishing between the two when studying current events. It covers the relative volatility of manufacturing output, retail sales, consumption and savings. The likelihood of time lags is explained through the relationship between output and employment. Lastly, it takes North Sea oil as an example of an event with implications throughout the rest of the economy.

3 Performance and policy
Looking at aspects of economic performance and the extent to which policy has had an impact upon them, this section covers investment, productivity, inflation and taxation.

4 Moving forward
Using the opening case study on the World Bank's theory of economic growth, this section outlines the components of economic success. It then goes on to define different kinds of problems and to consider what underlying variables may be

important. It reminds the student that policies have reflected the priorities of the political party in power at the time, and that there are some serious problems with data which make assessment of current trends difficult. The enquiry concludes with a brief look at the policies available and gives pointers towards the remaining four enquiries.

Pathways for enquiry

A survey of UK economic performance

There are a number of questions which can be examined in order to do this. These are some; there are many others.

➤ What are the criteria for 'success' in controlling the economy?

➤ What data will be needed from other sources to help shed light on the performance of the economy?

➤ Where are the data to be found?

➤ Have some years been better than others?

➤ What sorts of changes have taken place in the UK in recent years?

➤ Which of these changes happened as a result of some government policy?

➤ Why might we consider it important to control the economy?

➤ What policies can governments use to exert control over the economy?

➤ Why is it sometimes unclear what policy is likely to be most helpful?

➤ What would the government have had to do to reduce unemployment in 1989?

➤ Analyse the policy options in late 1993.* What drawbacks do they each have?

➤ With hindsight, which do you think would have been the right policy? Was this the one adopted?

*Any year could be picked but it is best to choose one in which the data indicate a clear-cut dilemma. In 1993 there was high unemployment, the recovery seemed rather slow, inflation was very low and politicians were talking about the need to help the recovery along with at least a neutral budget. However the PSBR was very high, and the chancellor actually introduced a substantial tax increase in the budget.

Hindsight will show whether the policy was wise. It may turn out that inflationary pressures were about to build up and further reflation would have worsened the situation.

A survey of two other countries' economic performance

To what extent have some countries performed well on some criteria and badly on others? Evaluate the significance of a high level of investment in promoting growth. Are savings significant in helping to generate growth? Is competition an important factor in the growth process?

Using aggregate supply and aggregate demand analysis

Whatever the state of the economy, the position can be analysed using aggregate demand and aggregate supply. Is there spare capacity? Is inflation accelerating? Is there growth with low inflation? What is the likely outcome of current trends.

An exploration of the impact of North Sea oil in the past, present and future

Falling imports after North Sea oil became available affected the exchange rate. The change in the exchange rate affected a) manufacturers and b) consumers. What will happen to UK growth rates if oil production falls further? What effect will the discovery of oil reserves off the Liverpool coast have? How have changes in the revenue generated by petroleum revenue tax affected the PSBR?

All these changes, except the last, can be analysed using supply and demand, exchange rate effects and the multiplier.

Testing the hypothesis that growth must be associated with rising productivity

Study output and productivity data for three countries over a period of at least a decade. What is the relationship between them? Does rising productivity always lead to growth of output? Are there any other elements in this process which ought also to be considered? Are the three countries you chose representative?

Useful resources

➤ The Nuffield *Student's Book*! This enquiry calls for a review of relevant past work and honing prior knowledge will be very worthwhile. Particular units upon which this option builds are 1/3; 3/2; 3/3 and 4/1.

➤ The Economist Schools Briefs, *Labour Market Economics*, number 1, *Labour Pains*, 12 February 1994

Enquiry 2: Can an open economy be controlled?

The selected evidence aims to provide a bird's-eye view of events in the UK economy in the period 1988 to 1993. This illustrates dynamically the problems of control when the business cycle has combined with other events to produce major changes in inflation and unemployment. It will be important to update this with similar observations, snapshots of the current economic problems and the policy response, taken every year or so. A stock of cuttings and articles in the classroom will be helpful.

Synopsis

1 The business cycle and macroeconomic stabilisation

This section takes a historical approach, starting with Keynes and the 1930s and moving on to demand management in the post-war period. It outlines the stop-go problem and the monetarist response. It concludes with a swift survey of the more recent dilemmas of macroeconomic policy.

2 Fiscal policy

A review of the effects of tax changes is followed by coverage of long-term trends in taxation and expenditure levels, and government borrowing.

3 Monetary policy

Opening with a brief survey of the nature of capital markets and financial institutions, this section covers the functions of the Bank of England and the link between monetary growth and price levels. The role of expectations is included as are time lags and the international dimension of interest rate policy.

4 Exchange rate policy

The international context is explored in more depth, covering the role of the ERM and the experience of France and the UK. Using theory with which students are already familiar, this section attempts to clarify the links between domestic macroeconomic policy and exchange rate policy.

5 Confidence, expectations and the financial markets

This is a short section highlighting the pressures which the financial markets can put on policy makers.

6 A disciplined approach

This section opens with a passage which will date quickly because it is about the November 1993 Budget. However, it raises important issues of long-term interest concerning the likelihood of inflation speeding up as the economy recovers. This is something which students will be able to observe. One hopes that students will begin to see the economy as a serial, in which fresh episodes are constantly unfolding. If they have been encouraged to develop their own predictions, they can see whether these are accurate before the course ends.

Comparisons can be made between, say, 1993 and 1996 or 1997. Was inflation slain? Did the UK kiss goodbye to its long-term prospects of growth? Did something quite unexpected happen which changed everyone's view of what was going on? What has happened to taxation and spending?

This section concludes with the important point that increased aggregate demand cannot for long reduce unemployment which is fundamentally structural in nature.

7 Some alternative possibilities

The final section looks briefly at the prospects of an independent central bank and European monetary union.

Pathways for enquiry

A survey of macroeconomic policy from the time at which the option book was written (early 1994) to the present

Fiscal, monetary and exchange rate policy will have undergone a number of changes in response to economic change and to political pressures. These can be analysed in terms of their effect on aggregate supply and demand, their effect on output, employment and inflation, and also on consumption, investment, exports and imports.

Information on this will need to have been collected from the media over a fairly long period so it would be necessary to start work on this some way ahead.

Investigating the time lags involved in the operation of monetary policy

This will require study of the data. The SECOS data-handling programme can demonstrate time lags on the Economic Background Data of the Nuffield Investigations and Data disk, or on Eureco. The stages of the process should be traced: a change in interest rates leads to a change in demand for loans and in consumption and investment spending, which, in turn, lead to a change in aggregate demand.

Studying the effects of the business cycle and macroeconomic policy on firms and households over a given time period

It seems likely that economic policy will continue to affect decision takers in widely different ways according to their circumstances. Select a firm or a family which has been affected by external economic events, and analyse the forces acting upon them and their response.

An analysis of the Budget

What are the current priorities and how did the chancellor approach them? What changes were made and what are their likely effects on people, firms and the economy?

Useful sources

➤ *The UK Economy* by the National Institute of Economic and Social Research (2nd edn, 1993), one of Heinemann's *Studies in the British Economy*, has useful chapters on fiscal and monetary policy.

➤ *The Inflation Report* and 'Bank Briefings', published quarterly, and fact sheets, all produced by the Bank of England, are useful sources of both data and current analyses. Available from The Bulletin Group, Economics Division, Bank of England, Threadneedle Street, London EC2R 8AH.

➤ A copy of the *Financial Times* should be bought for the classroom the day after the Budget, and kept. The chancellor's speech is printed in full and this will include a macroeconomic assessment which gives an up-to-date view of the government's philosophy. There is also much useful data on monetary and fiscal policy.

Enquiry 3: Can everyone prosper?

The focus of this enquiry is primarily on microeconomic polices which can contribute to productivity growth, competitiveness and employment creation. This area is less simple than it appears because certain policies are desirable for a whole range of reasons.

Synopsis

1 The growth process

The focus here is upon productivity growth and on the link between growth and trade. These strands lead to consideration of the elements of competitiveness, and the effects that inflation may have on this.

2 Structural change

This section highlights the difficulties which may occur when resources need to be reallocated. It reviews some evidence of skills' mismatch.

3 Policies which increase supply

Investment in physical and human capital, research and development and supply side policies in general are included here. The data cover evidence of UK performance to date.

4 The unemployment problem

This section covers the dimensions of the problem in the UK and, to a lesser extent, the EU, and the difficulties associated with long-term unemployment. Microeconomic policies which have been implemented are reviewed.

5 The outlook for the future

At the time of writing, the Uruguay Round had just been completed and this section briefly describes the likely implications for employment.

Pathways for enquiry

An investigation of current supply-side policy measures in force

The issues of current importance change over time and the nature of the measures in force changes to reflect that. Any such investigation should concentrate on recent governmental thinking. This pathway could include an assessment of microeconomic unemployment policies, evaluating their effectiveness and outlining possible alternatives.

A study of the process of structural change

Which industries are growing relatively (i.e. more than the average), which of them are declining absolutely (i.e. output is falling) and which of them are declining relatively (i.e. output is rising but by less than the average)? Assess the causes and the significance of the changes identified. What are their implications for people and for economic policy decisions?

A study of the effects of the Uruguay Round

The growth of trade and growth of output can be explored and their effects analysed in terms of import penetration, export growth and changes in employment opportunities.

Long-term unemployment and the policy response

Review the current scale of the problem. What policies are currently in place? Evaluate the effectiveness of these policies in relation to the size of the problem. Could more be done? What would be the opportunity cost of doing more? (This overlaps somewhat with the previously suggested investigation of supply-side policy measures in force.)

Useful sources

➤ *Unemployment and Job Creation* by Andy Beharrell (Macmillan, 1992)
➤ *UK Trade and Sterling* by Charles Smith (1992), one of Heinemann's *Studies in the British Economy*; Chapter 9 provides material on trade and supply-side policies.
➤ In the same series, *UK Unemployment* by Andrew Clark and Richard Layard, (2nd edn, 1993), provides thorough coverage of all aspects of unemployment.
➤ The Economist Schools Briefs, *Labour Market Economics*, number 5, *The Manufacturing Myth*, 19 March 1994 and *Investing in People*, number 6, 26 March 1994

Enquiry 4: Do all problems of control start in the labour market?

This is a difficult enquiry, taking students right to the frontier of our understanding of economic problems.

There is some evidence that, at the time of writing, conditions in the labour market may be changing. The rate of real earnings increase is lower than it has been for a long time. Productivity is rising and so are profits. The impact of this on the rate of inflation may be favourable. It may be possible for the UK to achieve a degree of competitiveness which makes it well placed to benefit from increased demand in export markets when the recession ends there. Also, unemployment started to fall much sooner after the end of the recession. The time lag may have changed in a fundamental way.

It is too soon to say what the effect of all this may be, but it provides a fine opportunity for students to investigate and analyse the changes taking place. The student option book can really only hint at the possibilities because more evidence is needed. This will have to be collected by teachers and students.

Synopsis

The opening evidence presents a range of viewpoints on pay, unemployment, technical change, labour market flexibility and inflation. These will help to define the scope of the enquiry from the outset.

1 How is pay determined?

Here, the approach to pay determination uses very basic theory, referring to the supply of, and demand for, labour, derived demand, elasticities and the possibilities of substituting capital for labour. The section goes on to discuss the effect of recession on the demand for labour and looks at pay determination in practical terms. Managerial pay and recent changes in the role of trade unions are included.

2 Inflation, expectations and sticky wages

The question here is why earnings have grown consistently in real terms, despite the presence of large numbers of unemployed people. The question is analysed by following events in the late 1980s and showing how monetary growth, low savings and tax cuts combined to raise demand, spending, prices and expectations of inflation. The end result was the sharp rise in interest rates which culminated in serious recession. This leads on to an exploration of the persistent nature of unemployment and the limited effect which long-term unemployment has on the level of pay settlements. The section

concludes with an analysis of the system of pay determination in the UK and other countries.

3 A more flexible labour market

The concept of an efficient labour market is explored, along with the sources of inflexibility or failure to adjust to new circumstances. Evidence of increasing flexibility in the UK is surveyed, together with the consequences for income distribution and job security.

4 Are there any solutions?

This is a very brief look at a range of possibilities, from cutting benefits to opting into the social chapter of the Maastricht Agreement.

Pathways for enquiry

Reviewing the labour market

Trace and record the changes since 1993 in employment, unemployment, productivity, inflation, real earnings and output. To what extent has the unemployment problem diminished?

To what extent have labour markets continued to become more flexible? What effect has this had on income distribution? How have the consequences generally affected different groups of people?

Expectations and inflation: reviewing the link

The statement that expectations of inflation were running at 4% per year in 1994 leads to the conclusion that pay increases might grow subsequently. This can be investigated by students. To what extent did expectations fail to adjust despite continuing lower than expected rates of inflation at that time? What can this tell us about the tendency of real wages to grow despite large numbers of unemployed? The Inflation Report carries data on expected inflation and earnings increases.

Reviewing the role of the trade unions

Trade unions are actively rethinking their role in the workplace. How has their role changed since the days of frequent industrial disputes in the 1970s? To what extent are unions now seeking to protect members' real incomes, even if this ends in job losses? Can unions influence job security?

Investigating the current competitiveness of UK producers

Examine the current data, including inflation relative to that of competing countries, exchange rates, productivity, unit costs, and changes in exports and imports. Assess the difficulties facing exporters and firms competing with imports. To what extent are the difficulties caused by pay settlements?

Useful sources

➤ *Mrs Thatcher's Economics: Her Legacy* by David Smith, Heinemann *Studies in the UK Economy* (1992); Chapter 5 on union law and the labour market.

➤ This will be superseded by *UK Current Economic Policy*, by David Smith (Heinemann, 1994).

➤ Also in the series, *Supply Side Economics* by Nigel Healey and Rosalind Levacic (1992) is useful.

➤ The Economist Schools Briefs, *Labour Market Economics*, number 3; *A bad case of arthritis*, 26 Febuary 1994.

➤ *Social Trends* (HMSO) has data on the number of part-time as against full-time employees.

➤ Trade unions will give information on their view of the economy and their role: Trade Union Congress, Congress House, Great Russell Street, London, WC1B 3LS.

Enquiry 5: Trade-offs and the global economy: what are the choices?

Parts of this option book are not easy to take in, especially Enquiries 2 and 4. Enquiry 5 introduces some new material but it also acts as an overview of the whole. Whereas students may have felt that they were only beginning to understand these previous chapters, now they have a chance to consolidate. In this enquiry the emphasis is less specifically on the UK. There is also an attempt to present policies which might be used

in the future to deal with intractable problems, rather than just to use those which have been employed in the past. There are hostages to fortune here: the future for this book may be the past by the time it is in use. It is better to risk dating than to be limited to generalities and beg for forgiveness when the inevitable happens.

Synopsis

The opening evidence stresses the interrelatedness of national economies within the world economy. It is no longer possible to imagine that any country's economy is functioning independently.

1 Trade-offs

A range of trade-offs is outlined, starting with the original Phillips relationship and the idea of NAIRU. The expectations-augmented Phillips curve is not mentioned as such, but it is expected that students will by now appreciate the role of expectations in a more intuitive way. Next, the equity/efficiency trade-off is looked at from the point of view of the association between labour market flexibility and increasing pay inequality. This is followed by a swift review of environmental trade-offs and of the trade-off between growth and the balance of payments. Because the objective is to gain an overview, all of these items are covered briefly.

Students may find it useful to refer at this point to Figure 6 on p. 372 of the *Student's Book*, which gives data on inflation and unemployment in the UK.

2 The policy choices

This section looks at party political solutions to the economic problems described and points out that many countries face similar problems. It then outlines the possibilities of policy packages to deal with a range of objectives.

3 What makes countries more interdependent?

Trade, capital movements and the activities of multinationals have all grown, making the world economy more and more of an integrated whole.

4 How do international institutions aid collaboration?

Starting with Bretton Woods, the framework of collaboration is described by tracing its development over the years, emphasising the IMF and the exchange rate system which has not previously been covered in any depth. The section then moves on to GATT and the need for a global approach to environmental measures. Finally, the need for macroeconomic policy co-ordination is explained, and the efforts of G7 and the possible role of the EU are outlined.

Pathways for enquiry

Looking at the relationship between inflation and unemployment

This relationship is very complex but if you think in terms of a short-run trade-off which operates against a background of varying levels of expected inflation, a pattern emerges. Studying the data since 1970, there have been periods of time when expectations of inflation accelerated rapidly. These have been followed by periods in which expectations were cooled by very depressed economic conditions. In between, there have been periods when the trade-off was clearly visible in the data. Identify the relevant periods. Describe the theoretical reasons for the trade-off and show what has happened to the relationship between inflation and unemployment.

Finding ways of heading off the environmental problem

Identify two current environmental problems for which changes in the tax system might be used to alter the allocation of resources in appropriate ways.

Assessing the contribution of the international organisations

Review the impact of the IMF, GATT or the EU. List the main changes which the organisation has brought about. Assess the extent to which member countries depend on these international structures. Try to imagine what might happen if they did not exist. Identify improvements in their operation which might be possible in the future.

This is a rather weighty suggestion and one which is bound to lead to speculative and perhaps vague conclusions. Despite this, it is probably worth some thought, because the international institutions are often taken for granted and their role underestimated.

Devising a policy package

Make a list of the four most urgent priorities in economic policy now. Put them in order of importance. Devise a policy package to tackle all of them, but emphasising the most important, and explain how it would work in detail. Explain what side effects the policy package will have and whether something (what?) may need to be done about them. Lastly, identify any likely political difficulties which might be encountered. Try to avoid taking a party political line. All political parties are prevented by traditional ideologies from considering policies on their merits. However, be aware that electorally unpopular policies are unrealistic. If a policy is very unpopular, think why, and, if it is really necessary, how it might be made less so. Do not waste time on proposals which would require a totally undemocratic form of government.

Updating the record

If you made chronological lists of major economic events while studying Stages 1/3 and 4/1, these should be brought up to date in the light of what you have learned during this option.

Useful sources

➤ *Mrs Thatcher's Economics: Her Legacy* by David Smith, Heinemann *Studies in the UK Economy*, (1992); Chapter 2, on monetarism and the control of inflation.

➤ In the same series, *Inflation* by David Heathfield (1992) has a chapter on the effect of expectations on inflation rates.

➤ *The European Union* by Brian Hill, Heinemann *Studies in the UK Economy* (1994), has a chapter on the impact of membership on the UK.

Option 3: Resources and Expansion: What are the limits to growth?

The option draws together a range of limitations which affect the functioning of businesses and economies. They are identified as tiers of constraints which range from those which affect individual firms to those which affect the entire world.

Firms have a broad range of limits upon them, which need careful strategic thinking if they are to be overcome. Beyond these, both firms and economies face limitations which will control our future if ignored.

The overall objective is to look forward in order to recognise what must be done in order to achieve a situation in which growth can continue without causing irreparable damage to the systems on which we depend.

By investigating the effect of political systems and the development of environmental thinking, the prospects for the future become clearer because the problems can be identified and solutions sought.

The solutions range from those which will occur as part of the market process, through ones in which the market can be used to good effect, to those where legislative control is the only solution.

The option as a whole deals with these limits in the context of the firm and the economy. Strategies for survival involve the firm in overcoming financial and other problems, and also international measures for safeguarding our long-term future.

'What are the limits to growth?' builds on the work of the stages. Both 'How do firms expand?' (3/1) and 'What makes an economy grow?' (3/2) are sources of introductory material. 'What is the impact of shock?' (4/2) and 'Can we plan for the future?' (4/3) both develop the theme and 'What happens in booms and slumps?' (4/1) identifies the macroeconomic processes which underlie some of the constraints.

Teaching this option

This option requires students to be aware of issues and events which are taking place during the course of their studies. The strategies companies use to extend their frontiers and the limitations which hinder both them and national economies in their search for growth are the common ground of the option. The most effective way of raising awareness is to collect newspaper articles, so that a store of information develops. Students should be asked to participate in this activity.

Newspaper articles from CD-ROM allow ready access to reasonably recent material. The identification of keywords which will produce appropriate articles is a skill which students need to develop.

Several of the books that have been recommended for the pathways for enquiry look at issues from a particular perspective. Students need to bear this in mind when using them because it is important to realise that there is also an alternative view.

Several books are useful for all the enquiries in this option. They are mainly annual publications which are available from large public libraries.

➤ *The World Development Report* (World Bank, OUP)
➤ *The Human Development Report* (UNDP, OUP)

The data from the *World Development Report* are available on disk as World Trends. Along with the Nuffield Investigations and Data disk, this is available from Statistics for Education, 5 Bridge Street, Bishops Stortford, Herts CM23 2JU.

There are several references to books by David Pearce, Kerry Turner and other members of the Centre for Social and Economic Research on the Global Environment (CSERGE). There are frequent updates, new publications and ideas coming from this group, so it is worth looking out for new titles.

Enquiry 1: Identifying the limits

Synopsis

The opening evidence provides a range of material which is designed to increase the awareness of students about factors which contain the development of firms and the economy as a whole. It is important to realise that constraints on firms and individuals are ultimately constraints on the economy.

1 The tiers of constraint

The text breaks the limits into four categories:

➤ **Company constraints** which stem from within the company and are associated with the running of the organisation in the market for its particular products.
➤ **Economic constraints** which result from the state of the national or international economy.
➤ **Resource constraints** which limit growth because many of the resources which we rely on are non-renewable and therefore cannot be replaced once used up.
➤ **External growth constraints** which are outcomes of growth but will limit future growth if not contained.

This categorisation assists in an understanding of the interrelationships between them because it demonstrates how actions in one field will have an impact on events in others.

2 Company constraints

This section identifies a variety of factors which may limit the expansion of a company. The following topics are included: organisational structure, production, marketing, finance and human resourcing. This creates a link with the stages.

3 Economic constraints

The economic constraints section follows a similar pattern of identifying relevant material from the stages which needs to be applied in this context. The following topics are included: unemployment, inflation, international trading problems, core and periphery (or regional problems) and trade-offs in decision making.

4 Resource constraints

Non-renewable resources are the issue at stake here. If all were renewable, their consumption would not be a problem. From work earlier in their school career many students will be aware of the difficulties. The meaning and interpretation of reserves is discussed using oil and gas as an example. The effect that scarcity has on price is raised in order to develop an understanding of how the market may lead to conservation as resources become increasingly scarce.

5 External growth constraints

In this section, problems which arise because of economic growth are investigated. The growth of production at the individual plant level has externalities, but the growth process as a whole also has its own externalities.

Population has increased as death rates have fallen. As people's standards of living have risen, they have started looking for a better way of life. This has led to rapidly growing cities in which many live in squalor.

Increasing demand has led to increasing pollution. The joint activities of industry have raised threats of acid rain, thinning of the ozone layer and the greenhouse effect. The trade-off which exists between current and future production is explained using production possibility frontiers.

Pathways for enquiry

Company constraints

The Nuffield Investigations and Data disk contains a case study of Laura Ashley at the time when it was in trouble. The material was used earlier in the course but this time the business can be examined from a different starting point. It is a useful way of identifying the factors which cause problems. Students can take a list of potential problems and interrogate the data accordingly. Strategies are suggested in the accompanying guide.

Any company which is currently confronted by problems is a useful source of material for the identification of constraints. In the text there are several examples of such companies. Problems may be very wide ranging but they usually stem from one of the categories discussed above. Newspaper reports will be a useful source of examples because many companies will not wish to discuss their difficulties with outsiders.

The two books on corporate strategy, which are listed below, are useful references. Their indexes will assist searches for specific types of problems.

Economic constraints

The current state of the economy will determine the methods used to identify these constraints. Recession generally imposes more limits, so case study material may sometimes be more relevant than contemporary research. The Economic Background section of the Nuffield Investigations and Data disk will again prove useful.

A CD-ROM search of the newspapers, using words such as 'company', 'recession', 'growth', 'investment', etc. will produce a range of useful articles.

Resource constraints

The important factor in this section is to identify which resources are renewable and which are non-renewable. Students will generally be well informed on the issues

because they featured earlier in the course, as well as in their general education. By looking at the raw materials which are used in producing a range of manufactured products, the distinction should become clear.

External growth constraints

This covers a considerable range of examples of ways in which growth constrains the future. Students should be encouraged to identify others.

Individuals or groups of students might follow particular aspects of the debate in order to present their findings to the rest. In this way, a broader investigation can be carried out in the time available.

Population growth and mobility might be investigated in one country while correlating the pattern with growth. The World Trends Database on SECOS has some investigations in Study 2: World Population, which relate to population growth and density. In Study 4: Global Urbanisation, the problems of urban concentration are considered.

The effect of pollution on a specific economy, especially as the source may be in other countries, is interesting. For example, Scandinavia receives damaging pollution from Western Europe and North America.

Varying estimates of the damage caused by pollution on a world-wide basis make an interesting comparison. The predictions vary substantially and show how pessimists and optimists look at the possibilities for the future.

Having explored the material, the students can be asked to identify the trade-offs. By taking the roles of affected individuals, they will see the problems which may arise more clearly. Libraries now have many texts on pollution and the environment but *Environmental Economics* (details below) is particularly useful. Specific national information is available from embassies of countries which are affected.

Useful sources

The following materials can be used in this enquiry to identify the source of problems:

➤ *Exploring Corporate Strategy* by Gerry Johnson, Kevan Scholes (Prentice Hall, 1993)

➤ *Corporate Strategy* by Igor Ansoff (Penguin Books, 1987)

➤ *Environmental Economics* by R. Kerry Turner, David Pearce and Ian Bateman (Harvester Wheatsheaf, 1994)

➤ *Statistics for Education,* Nuffield Investigations and Data disk

Environmental organisations, such as Friends of the Earth (which has a publications catalogue) and Greenpeace, are useful sources of information.

➤ Friends of the Earth, 26 Underwood Street, N1 7JT. Tel: 0171–490 1555

➤ Greenpeace, Information Deptartment, Canonbury Villas, London N1. Tel: 0171–354 5100

➤ The Green Party, 10 Station Parade, London SW12 9AZ

➤ The main political parties all have statements on the environment.

Enquiry 2: Use or abuse?

Synopsis

The overall objective of this enquiry is to identify balanced growth and sustainability.

The opening evidence provides a range of opinions about what countries in different political systems are trying to achieve and how they go about it. Economics is both used and abused in the selection of material. It demonstrates how the concepts must be used in a broad context if they are to be put to good effect.

1 What is balanced growth?

The first section compares the reality of growth in Scandinavia with communist USSR in order to investigate the meaning of balanced growth. The idea of sustainability is introduced.

2 Pathways to growth

This looks at how different political structures have been responsible for creating limits to growth. The rationale of the capitalist model is explained and a Marxist critique is given, which is used to identify some flaws in the system. The critique itself is subject to some criticism. The merits and demerits of command economies and socialist and co-operative systems are outlined.

3 The end of an illusion

The three systems discussed above have all been a source of problems in the way that they have achieved growth. This section uses case study examples to demonstrate the ways in which these failures have come about.

Mexico City, as it was at the time of the conquistadores, is compared with the polluted sprawling urban city that exists today. The effects of radio–active effluent from the defence industry of the USSR shows the order of priorities that existed in the country. Tanzania's attempts at creating co-operative villages in order to raise health and education standards and encourage a controlled level of growth are evaluated.

4 Sustainability: avoiding abuse

The many varying definitions of sustainability are compared here. The work of David Pearce and others at CSERGE (Centre for Social and Economic Research on the Global Environment) is used to show the varying levels of sustainability which can be attained.

An equation, which shows how much our natural and manufactured capital is being depleted and degraded, demonstrates how sustainability can be measured.

Pathways for enquiry

Markets and monopolies

The Marxist challenge, that a market economy will lead to monopoly, can be researched by looking at the size of large companies, their profits and referrals to the

Monopolies and Mergers Commission. The trends in the number of small firms is quoted in the text but this can be updated from the Department of Trade and Industry. Do not forget that the figure will be greatly influenced by the general state of the economy, which provides another insight into economic constraints.

➤ Small Firms' Statistics Unit, Department of Trade and Industry, 2nd Floor, St Mary's House, Sheffield, S1 4PQ. Tel: (0114) 259 7475

Issues in Eastern Europe
The changing pattern as former Eastern Europe moves into the market economy will be interesting to follow. Questions are continually being asked about the changes that are taking place as a result of some countries' wishes to draw closer to Europe.

Find out what measures are being taken by one of these countries to meet the standards of environmental protection which are required of members of the EU.

➤ CD-ROM searches and *The Human Development Report* are possible sources for such searches.

What is meant by sustainability?
Sustainability is the subject of much environmental writing and has widely different interpretations. An evaluation of the different interpretations in terms of their effect on current lifestyles would help students to understand their implications.
➤ It is easy to claim that sustainability means passing on all non-renewable resources but what does this mean for today?
➤ What trade-offs are to be made to achieve different levels of sustainability?
➤ Can an equally beneficial effect be achieved by other strategies?

This will lead students to seek solutions that will prepare them for future investigations.

Useful sources

➤ *Our Common Future*, Chapters 1 and 2, World

Commission on Environment and Development (OUP, 1987)
➤ *Blueprint for a Green Economy*, Chapters 1 and 2 by David Pearce, Anil Markandya, Edward B. Barbier (Earthscan, 1989)
➤ *Blueprint 3*, Pages 28–39, by David Pearce, R. Kerry Turner, Timothy O'Riordan (Earthscan, 1994)

Enquiry 3: Strategies for survival

Synopsis

The opening evidence looks at the range of solutions to problems that confront firms, including ways of reducing the external effects of their activities. The focus moves to looking at the effects of these externalities and at strategies which governments might use to overcome them.

1 Inter-relationships
This enquiry opens with an identification of the inter-relationships which exist between the actions of companies, governments and individuals. It is important for students to realise that there are knock-on effects from almost every activity and that these must be considered when strategies and policies are decided.

2 Corporate strategy for survival
The second section identifies a variety of ways in which firms attempt to overcome potential limits to their future development. It incorporates mergers, demergers, restructuring, technological change and a short case study about Benetton, which demonstrates how a strategy may combine several of these factors. 'Ten tips for turning the corner' was originally written to give firms advice on overcoming the effects of recession but is valuable advice for any company seeking growth. The last part of this section shows how looking after the environment can lead to growth.

3 International strategies for survival
This section looks at the origins of environmental

thought and the developments over the last 30 years. There are two sources of thought. Those who followed Malthusian ideas came up with a doomsday scenario, whereas those who based their thinking on Ricardo sought ways of using the market to adjust events in order to overcome the problems.

The terms ecocentrism and technocentrism are introduced to demonstrate the range of views. The former involves extreme preservationism and the latter means that the market and technological development will negate the problems of scarcity. These ideas represent the opposite ends of the spectrum and most views fall somewhere between the two.

4 The national position
This section puts the UK into the context of the international environmental picture. It asks how it has responded to the Earth summit and European standard–setting?

5 The role of the individual
The role of the individual has been significant in these developments so the final section shows how individuals have influenced the situation. It also looks briefly at why interest wanes.

Pathways for enquiry

Corporate strategy
In order to understand the formation of such strategy, students might select an industry with which they are familiar and draw up a diagram showing growth vectors in order to devise a 'strategic portfolio' for a specific company. This involves looking at the strengths of the company and suggesting product areas into which it might move.

Having done this, a 'competitive strategy' should be put together showing how the company plans to approach the market place. How would they attempt to sell the products in this new market? The various examples in the text should provide useful support.

While doing this, they should think carefully about the

limits which have already been discussed and create strategies accordingly.

Keep an eye open for companies which are moving into new areas and watch their progress and tactics. This information would provide a good model for students to use in their work.

'Strategy is when you are out of ammunition, but keep right on firing so the enemy won't know.' (Anon)
Identify a company which is in trouble. Use a current example from the media or find one from the past from the papers on CD-ROM. Look for the causes of its problems and decide what limits are constraining its future. How should it move ahead? What strategies can be devised to achieve the objectives?

This should take students beyond the material in the text as these situations are usually multi-faceted and therefore may require a broader interpretation. This is particularly useful for helping students to see the inter-relationships between the actions of a company.

The first two books in the resource section will assist with back-up information.

Evaluating other environmental perspectives
In the text, a range of different opinions about the environment and our relationship to the limits of growth have been identified. They represent the main trends in thought and are concerned with the practice that we see developing in governments around the world.

There are, of course, other strands of thought which students may wish to explore. In the resources section several books are suggested, which fall into this category. In using them, students should remember to apply their economic knowledge to propositions in order to test their validity.

They could be asked to work in groups and make an evaluative presentation of a particular view of our environmental future.

Survey of UK and European policy

The UK has to achieve certain targets of environmental standards in a wide range of fields. The press often tells us of our failures but comparisons often show that others are as bad, if not worse. Is this true?

The Department of the Environment has information about UK targets, what we have achieved and what the targets are. The European Commission can provide information about Europe's targets. Addresses are given below. Newspapers on CD-ROM may also assist.

Individual responsibility

There is a strong suspicion that the consumer responds more fervently to the need for care of the environment when incomes are secure. Is this true?

A survey might be used to show how individuals respond. A questionnaire needs to take into account:
➤ Behaviour in the current economic climate
➤ Behaviour in an alternative situation
➤ Whether people will pay above the odds for products which are demonstrated to do less damage
➤ How they feel about existing 'green' products and their marketing
➤ Any other interesting points?

Remember the rules for dealing with questionnaires, which were explained in Unit 3/1.

Useful sources

➤ *Exploring Corporate Strategy* by Gerry Johnson, Kevan Scholes (Prentice Hall, 1993)
➤ *Corporate Strategy* by Igor Ansoff (Penguin Books, 1987)
➤ *The Limits to Growth* by D. Meadows et al. (Earthscan, 1972)
➤ *Beyond the Limits* by D. Meadows et al. (Earthscan, 1992)
➤ *The Growth Illusion* by Richard Douthwaite (Hartland/Green Books, 1992)
➤ *The First Global Revolution* by King and Schneider (Simon and Schuster, 1992)
➤ *Staying Alive* by V. Shiva (Zed Books, 1992)

➤ *Think Globally, Act Locally* by K. Coates (Spokesman, 1992)

➤ EU information comes from The Commission of The European Communities, 8 Storeys Gate, London SW1. Tel: 0171-973 1992

➤ Department of the Environment, 2 Marsham Street, London SW1P 3EB, Tel: 0171-267 0929

Enquiry 4: What is the role of the market?

Synopsis

The opening evidence sets out several perspectives on the role of the market in the environment. Some demonstrate its success and others its failure. The use of controls is also represented, both in terms of why they are needed and their effects when imposed.

The evidence presents students with a selection of ideas which demonstrate the ways in which the market can and cannot be put to use, as well as the human response to regulation.

1 Striving for success

This section shows how companies can use the market effectively to push out their limits. It uses Fairy Liquid as an example because, by quite traditional marketing techniques, it has succeeded in winning a much larger share of the market for washing up liquids. Other efforts are, however, less benign.

2 Why does it all go wrong?

When access is open, problems occur because there is no price to limit overconsumption. The depletion of fish stocks is used as an example. Open access is also the source of problems with acid rain, the ozone layer, global warming, etc.

3 Can the market curb pollution?

Various market measures of environmental control

are explained in this section. Green taxes are explored and their appropriate application discussed. Tradeable permits receive the same treatment and are exemplified with a case study on the control of fishing in New Zealand. They have the advantage that they put a price on resources that have been regarded as free in the past.

4 Energy: a source of the problem?

This section concentrates on the energy industry as it has often been quoted as the main source of many of the problems. The problems are first discussed and then solutions are sought. The workings and effects of a carbon tax are explored. This includes a look at the impact on the macroeconomy and the objective of delinking energy use from economic growth.

5 Command and control

Where there is open access to resources, the market is difficult to apply so controls have to be used. Many administrators prefer controls but they are less efficient economically. The effectiveness of controls is also considered. Administrators of regulations can become so involved with the industry they control that they start to adjust their thinking in accordance. This is known as 'regulatory capture'.

6 Markets, governments and the environment

Governments are subject to political pressures and policies are often affected by this. In the USA, petrol prices are a sensitive issue, whereas, in France, agriculture is high on the agenda.

This section looks at the interweaving of political needs and environmental pressures.

7 Who's cleaning up?

The final section shows how some companies have turned the environmental problem to their benefit as the market for both goods and services in this field grows.

Pathways for enquiry

Markets: the good and the bad

Identifying ways in which the market can be put to use to push out the limits or to cause harm, shows how powerful the process can be. Using newspapers on CD-ROM, students can gather examples of companies which have used the market effectively to gain, as in the Fairy Liquid case study in the text. They can also look for ways in which companies might create externalities in their use of the market.

Words such as companies, profits, marketing, new markets, strategies, may be useful in the first search. Companies, pollution, rivers, water, air, filters, etc. will assist with the second.

Energy: company conservation

During the course, a class will have used several companies in their investigative work. Their resources could now be pooled to carry out a survey of these companies to find out whether any change has taken place in their energy consumption relative to output. In what ways has this been achieved? Are there any plans for the future? Is any change driven by cost or a wider motive?

Energy: household conservation

The group might look at household energy consumption. What has happened to the size of bills relative to changes in price? Is demand elastic? Has an increase in price led to more insulation or the purchase of electrical goods which claim to be energy-saving? The local electricity company may need to be contacted to find out about price changes.

Controls on pollution

While companies are being interviewed about energy use, they could also be asked if any environmental protection laws affect them. What is the effect on costs? Did they have to install special equipment? Did they have to change the type of inputs, packaging, etc.?

Look in *Yellow Pages* to see if there are any companies in the locality which have benefited from stricter rules on the environment. Waste management firms, pollution control equipment (filters etc.) makers, environmental consultants, may all be willing to discuss their business. When did they start their business? What was the gap in the market that they observed? How had it been created? How has legislation helped them? Where are their markets? What are the trends?

Do controls distort?

In the text, the effect that the CAP has on farming is discussed. Use this as a model to look at other legislation to identify ways in which controls may create their own externalities. Chapter 3 in *Costing the Earth* by Frances Cairncross, which is listed below, shows a variety of ways in which controls have side effects. They provide an international dimension to the problem.

Useful sources

➤ *Environmental Economics* by R. Kerry Turner, David Pearce and Ian Bateman, Harvester (Wheatsheaf, 1994)
➤ *Blueprint for a Green Economy*, Chapter 7, by David Pearce, Anil Markandya, Edward B. Barbier (Earthscan, 1989)
➤ *Costing the Earth* by Frances Cairncross (Harvard Business School Press, 1993)
➤ *Economic Policy Towards The Environment* by Dieter Helm (Blackwell, 1992)

Enquiry 5: Are the limits insuperable?

Synopsis

The opening evidence combines ways in which the limits are being pushed forward, with comments on the need for care in future developments. It demonstrates the disparity between the views held by different people on sustainability. Governments, in particular, may view their activities as sustainable, while others do not.

1 A pessimist's view and its downfall

Malthus is used in order to identify the ways in which the limits can be extended. By demonstrating how the world changed, an understanding can be reached about how his prognosis was never fulfilled.

2 Moving towards sustainability

Government has an important role to play in the achievement of an integrated policy on the environment. However, the problems of its structure show why making this work is so difficult. Despite the problems, the UK is demonstrated to be weakly sustainable by using an equation which compares how much investment is taking place with the amount of environmental depletion and degradation. It is explained that this is not yet adequate but that the country is moving towards greater sustainability.

3 The impact of technology

The optical fibre is used to show how technology can have a major impact on the limits to growth. Not only does it reduce the use of copper but it allows people to work in different ways which also reduce pressure on the environment. Companies benefit as well because costs can be reduced.

4 The rise in productivity

Increasing productivity assists in pushing out the limits because more can be made using fewer resources. This process has been demonstrated throughout history.

5 The trend to services

As economies become more developed, there is a shift away from manufacturing industries to services. This is certainly linked to the relative costs of labour in different parts of the world but it also reflects the fact that, as people become more affluent, they want to buy more services. This may help to spread the use of non-renewable resources over a longer time period.

6 Alleviating poverty

Poverty has serious implications for environmental degradation in both urban and rural situations. By increasing equity, environmental damage will be reduced. There is strong evidence that pollution falls as income levels rise, so the reduction of poverty has an important role to play in delinking growth and pollution.

7 Counting the costs and benefits

Earlier in the course, cost–benefit analysis was discussed. In this section a variety of alternative methods is introduced. These provide students with different criteria for assessing the relative merits of new developments.

8 Achieving the unachievable

In order to evaluate the process, the costs and benefits which are incurred are important. In all the changes which are necessary for continued growth, there are trade-offs. At the extreme, it is suggested that the standard of living in the developed world should fall so that that of the rest of the world can rise. This is generally accepted as impossible. At a simpler level, is the trade-off between CFCs for refrigeration in the developing world and skin cancer in the developed world, acceptable?

The enquiry is completed with a look at the responsibility of companies for the environment and how this has to be balanced with the need for competitiveness through the market.

Figure 5.11 shows how some of these inter-relationships work.

Pathways for enquiry

Moving to sustainability

By using Figure 5.1, students can develop a practical framework for generating sustainability. They need to identify the measures which should be carried out to achieve the requirements of each box in the diagram.

Technological development

The example of optical fibres demonstrates how technology can push out the horizon by saving resources as well as permitting economic activity to range beyond what was imagined a decade ago.

What other examples are there of such developments?

What has happened to productivity?

Changes in productivity could be investigated by looking at one local firm or by using data. If a group of students is working on this, a combination of the two methods would lead to some useful comparisons. Do local firms or farms match national and international data? How do service industries compare with manufacturing industries?

If your area has a limited range of organisations, data might be traded with other schools and colleges, through the Network.

Why think about tomorrow when you have to survive today?

Much of the developing world is creating its own limits by the environmental problems that result from poverty. The problems may not simply be because of the way of life of indigenous people but also because of the pressures that are created by a country's development. The problem is therefore wide ranging.

Students might investigate the issue by finding examples, identifying the implications and looking for solutions. The final question is – what effect does the problem and its solutions have on the limits to growth in the short and long run?

Suggested examples: the building of a dam to provide electricity to growing industry and urban areas; farming marginal land; collecting wood to burn for cooking.

Julian Burger's book, listed below, gives many examples of the effects of development on indigenous people.

Growth and the service sector

Investigation 3:4 in Study 3 of The Word Trends Database on SECOS compares growth in economies with the development of the service sector. Students can identify the pattern and therefore draw conclusions as to whether this development provides hope for overcoming the limits.

Are the environmentalist's dream and the capitalist's drive compatible?

Using the diagram in Figure 5.11 and the extract from the speech by Sir John Collins, the Chair and Chief Executive of Shell, students should develop an argument which confirms or denies the question. In it, they should identify reasons why the limits to growth are either insuperable or not and explain how they perceive the future, using the ideas of economics and business which they have encountered in the course.

Useful sources

➤ *The Worldly Philosophers* by Robert Heilbroner (Penguin Books, 1991). Malthus and Ricardo are both discussed in Chapter 4 of this readable book.

➤ *Blueprint 3* Chapters 1 and 12, by David Pearce, R. Kerry Turner, Timothy O'Riordan (Earthscan, 1994)

➤ *Human Development Report 1993*
 – or subsequent (OUP)

➤ *Economic Analysis of the Environmental Impacts of Development Projects* by John Dixon et al. (Earthscan, 1987)

➤ *Report from the Frontier* by Julian Burger (Zed Books, 1987)

➤ *A New World Order* by Paul Ekins (Routledge, 1992)

➤ *Economic Values and the Natural World* by David Pearce (Earthscan, 1993)

➤ *World Development Report 1993*
 – or subsequent – (OUP)

➤ *The Environmental Audit and Business Strategy* by G. Ledgerwood et al. (Financial Times/Pitman, 1992)

➤ World Trends Database on SECOS, Statistics for Education

Option 4: Competition and Control: Who has power in the market?

Few markets even approach perfect competition. Wherever trade and exchange take place there are market imperfections which give either the buyer or the seller, or both, an element of market power. This option studies the ways in which market power manifests itself.

The market for goods and services forms an important part of the area of investigation, but market power also develops in the markets for factors of production. So power in the labour and capital markets also figures here.

Sometimes market power is the end result of collaboration between companies. The ways in which collaboration takes place are studied. Later, the measures taken by governments to prevent the abuse of market power are examined. A third strand in the subject concerns the way individuals can influence what happens in the market place.

Business, consumers and the government are the main players in a range of market situations and students should be encouraged to view events from various perspectives. There is considerable opportunity to transfer concepts from one situation to another and students will benefit from making these connections.

Sometimes the case study material which is available in this field generates a sense of real excitement. The inventive, and sometimes devious, activities of entities which are powerful in the market place create stories which seem larger than life. If the institutional or legal details have begun to seem tedious, it is time to get back to the real world and find out how the market is actually working.

Teaching this option

This option builds upon the content of the earlier stages and students will need to refer to their earlier studies. Particularly relevant areas of study from previous units include production and marketing, types of markets, competition, normal and super-normal profit, the fundamentals of price theory, the labour market, corporate culture, the importance of stakeholders and the role of the government. However, this particular option also really requires a good working knowledge of all four stages and students will benefit if they conscientiously revise as much as they can by way of preparation. Particular attention might be given to revising Stages 1 and 2 thoroughly, also Unit 3/1.

Because there is a real need to look at individual firms while studying this option, there will be heavy reliance on local business links for primary data, and on newspaper and journal sources for secondary data. CD-ROM is likely to be important as a source. Existing links with firms may be exploited, using student familiarity with the general nature of the business and building on it to explore issues of specific relevance to this option.

There are a number of case studies in *Business Case Studies* by Ian Marcousé with David Lines, (Longman, 1990) and also in the 2nd edition (1994) which are of relevance to this option. Some are mentioned specifically in 'useful sources', but there are many others which could be profitably used.

Chapter 5 of *The Culture of Contentment* by J. K. Galbraith (Sinclair-Stevenson, 1992) gives an interesting and critical view of the nature of markets as they actually are. It is not of particular relevance to any one enquiry but will provide stimulating background reading for able or thoughtful students.

Because this is a joint economics and business option, there are times when the best source is an A level text on one subject or the other.

Enquiry 1: What is market power?

Synopsis

1 Market types

The enquiry opens by looking at different types of market within any economy and begins to look at how businesses behave. It encourages students to look back at their work in the earlier stages and consolidate their ideas. It introduces monopolistic competition. This is important in terms of describing a commonly found market situation, and students will benefit from relating its features to local businesses.

2 How is market power measured?

Ways of measuring concentration are examined. The influence of individual businesses and how they may abuse their power are covered. The section goes on to look at how individual markets may be defined and the relevance of elasticities. The role of the government in curbing market power is introduced, but not in any detail, as this topic is the subject matter of Enquiry 5.

3 Barriers to entry

This section considers the problems facing new businesses and why they cannot launch into new markets without considerable research. It explores the relationship between barriers to entry and economies of scale. It encourages students to view competition as a hindrance to new businesses and prepares the way for considering anti-competitive activities. It concludes with brief views on contestable markets and control over supply.

4 The use of price as a way of competing

Pricing strategies are the focus of this section, which draws considerably upon earlier work. Students will need to spend time relating the information given here to what they see going on around them. Demand-based, cost-based and competition-based pricing are looked at in some detail and price leadership and price wars are included.

5 Power, performance and success

Michael Porter's work on competitive advantage is reviewed here.

Pathways for enquiry

It is possible to consider a range of market situations, exploring the degree of market power and the reasons for it in each case. Initially, the data in the book may be used, with additional data available in the classroom. Then the main focus should be upon a local company, perhaps one which has already been studied. It may well be possible to combine teaching objectives from several enquiries by focusing on one local firm and pursuing a number of lines of enquiry.

Investigating the degree of competition faced by video rental shops

Start out by considering a hypothetical case, using the case study material in the opening evidence, then go on to think about an actual local shop. The nature of competition between video rental shops is more complex than it at first appears. In particular, the significance of imperfect information should be considered.

The Post Office

Consideration of the question of how far the Post Office is able to use its monopoly position is an interesting one. Privatisation may have little effect on this aspect of its operations. How much competition does the Post Office letter and parcel delivery service actually face? What effect has competition had on its organisation? How might it develop in the future?

Defining substitutes

Investigate the competition and the extent to which the company's products have substitutes. It is important to realise that all products have substitutes, albeit some of them not very close.

It is possible to consider the extent to which consumers regard one product as a substitute for another. The purpose here is to understand the amount of consumer loyalty associated with their purchasing decisions. Identify five or six people who have purchased a particular product and investigate their attitude towards it, trying to discover why the consumers bought it. Issues of interest could be:

➤ Image
➤ Price
➤ Availability
➤ Colour
➤ Reputation.

As a conclusion, it should be possible to ascertain the extent to which a competing product would have served these customers equally well or whether consumers see little substitutability between products. The outcome should be reports on a range of products, some of which, by virtue of their own intrinsic features and of the nature of competing products, have a degree of monopoly power in the market. Group discussion of the outcome will enable students to share their findings.

Price war at *The Sun* and the *Daily Mirror*
In order to follow the course of a price war, investigate what has happened to the market share of the following newspapers since the price war of 1993: *The Sun*, *Daily Mirror*, *The Times* and the *Independent*. From this information can you say whether the price-cutting exercise was a success? What other information, besides market share, would be needed in order to judge whether the price cuts were a success?

An investigation of CD pricing policies
Recent progress in the debate on CD prices can be followed using CD-ROM. Why do the producers and the retailers take the positions they do? The Nuffield Investigations and Data disk has information on the recorded music industry which can be used for background.

A national company: examining price and non-price strategies for competing
Many of the most interesting stories come from large oligopolistic businesses operating in national or international markets. CD-ROM may be the best source. Unilever, Coca-Cola, IBM and many others may provide topical material.

A closer look at De Beers
The outstanding example of control of supply is the De Beers story. This provides an opportunity to analyse the components of a particular kind of market power, focusing on the control of price through control on quantity sold.

Useful sources

➤ *Readings in Economics*, Book 1, by R. Rees and R. E. Baxter (Collins, 1984) contains the full version of the De Beers story. It has a number of other useful case studies as well, including the Prisoner of War Camp story in full. Although it is now out of print, it should still be available in libraries.
➤ *Business Case Studies*, by Ian Marcousé with David Lines (Longman, 1990) Case Study 47, Ford's Model T, is a classic example of price competition.
➤ 'Barriers to Entry' by Geoffrey Myers, in *Economics and Business Education*, the Quarterly Journal of the EBEA, Autumn 1993.
➤ *The Essence of Business Economics* by Joseph G. Nellis and David Parker (Prentice Hall, 1992); Chapter 4 on competition, especially pages 92–98 on competitive advantage, and Chapter 6 on pricing. This is quite advanced and assumes a fair knowledge of microtheory but is very useful and unusual in using the two subjects together.

Enquiry 2: How do businesses become powerful?

This enquiry examines all the component parts of business success, linking success to the development of market power. Gaining the edge over competing firms often means either reducing costs or, through marketing, enhancing the desirability of the product.

Synopsis

1 Relationships with suppliers
In recent years the nature of relationships with

suppliers has changed. There is now much less emphasis on buying from the cheapest source and much more on creating reliable long-term relationships with supplier companies so that strategic planning is facilitated. The nature of these relationships is explored and the growth of subcontracting is also covered.

2 How businesses collaborate in the market

In many situations businesses would prefer to co-operate rather than compete. This section examines ways in which businesses can co-operate in order to earn higher profits. It covers collusion and tacit agreement, restrictive practices, mergers and takeovers and joint projects.

3 Striving for profits and growth

A major factor in business success concerns its production strategies. This section provides a link between sourcing issues and marketing issues and covers Just-In-Time (JIT), kaizen and quality issues. Employee involvement is mentioned but not covered in detail until Enquiry 4. The section concludes with a brief consideration of multinationals.

4 Marketing strategies

Students can develop their existing understanding of marketing strategies in order to grasp how business may seek to move beyond the reach of the competition. This enquiry takes the marketing mix further than students have previously gone, outlining some strategies for market analysis and development. Legal protection of new products is covered briefly.

The Nintendo case study has a useful integrating function as it takes in production abroad, new product development, oligopoly, complementary pricing, product differentiation, product life cycles, innovation and doubtless other concepts too. It demonstrates the way in which a company may have much potential market power yet still be hemmed in by very competitive forces.

Pathways for enquiry

A local investigation

Students may wish to build on their existing knowledge of a local firm, developing their understanding of it through a range of supplementary questions.

Some areas for investigation:
➤ What are the key factors that influence the success of this business?
➤ How many of these are within the control of the organisation?
➤ Investigate how the employees are organised in the production process.
➤ Do employees have control over their own production systems? What responsibility do they have for quality? If so, are there any problems with transferring so much power to the employees within a business? Isn't it really the manager's job to ensure quality is maintained and the costs kept under control?
➤ Are contractors being used for some of the work?
➤ Is the company co-operating with any other business? Are there advantages for consumers in this?
➤ Which areas of the marketing mix have and have not been addressed by the business? Can you determine why?

The scope of this investigation is potentially huge and teachers may wish to define it much more tightly. Alternatively, it could be allowed to become large and extended to cover more than this one enquiry.

The national context

Besides knowing what happens within a business, it is important to find out what has happened within the private sector as a whole.
➤ Investigate why the number of mergers declined in the early 1990s.
➤ Find examples of companies which diversified, companies which developed a stronger focus, and companies which developed strong export lines.
➤ Can high profits be justified if they finance the launch of new products that benefit consumers?
➤ The UK government is very proud of its ability to persuade Japanese companies to invest in the UK,

particularly in Wales. Is the Welsh Office right to be proud of the fact that overseas companies wish to invest in the UK?

➤ Are MNCs only attracted to countries with low labour costs?

Students may split into groups or pairs to investigate just one of these questions, reporting back to the full group at the end. There is extensive case study material in the book which may be found helpful for these questions.

Useful sources

➤ *Business Case Studies* by Ian Marcousé with David Lines, 2nd edn (Longman, 1994) case study 38, 'Kaizen – continuous improvement at OKI'. A more detailed version of the Marlborough story is provided in case study 84, 'Marlborough and market power'.

➤ *Applied Economics* by Alan Griffiths and Stuart Wall, (Longman, 1993); Chapter 5, on mergers and acquisitions and Chapter 9, Pricing in Practice.

➤ *Multinationals* by Richard Crum and Stephen Davies (Heinemann, 1991).

➤ *Competition Policy* by Paul Bennett and Martin Cave (Heinemann, 1991) has a chapter on anti-competitive practices.

➤ On marketing, *The Marketing Edge* by Tony McBurnie and David Clutterbuck (Penguin, 1987), especially pages 146–55, is very suitable for students.

➤ *Trouble Shooter* by John Harvey Jones with Anthea Massey (BBC, 1990).

➤ Market shares can be investigated using data on the music and car industries from the Nuffield Investigations and Data disk.

Enquiry 3: What powers do consumers have?

This enquiry considers the role of the consumer within the framework of market forces. It looks at how pressure groups and legislation try to even up the unequal relationship between buyers and sellers in the market. It goes on to consider how

society may be protected through public pressure from environmentally damaging decisions.

Synopsis

1 Consumer sovereignty

The section opens with a reference to Adam Smith and the economic theory and goes on to consider the impact of consumer sovereignty in the real world of marketing strategies and producer power. It introduces the concept of monopsony and examines the balance between genuine market orientation and the kind of market power which may adversely affect the consumer.

2 Consumer power and pressure groups

The concept of a pressure group is explained and the relevance of pressure groups to consumer issues is considered. German recycling policies are used as an example of the outcome of political pressure.

3 Consumers, society and the environment

This looks at environmental issues from the point of view of society as a whole and shows how both pressure groups and market forces may have a role to play in bringing about change.

4 Consumer rights

The legislation protecting consumers is covered in brief.

5 Consumer power or consumer preferences

Using the debate about road transport as a focus, this section makes the point that market forces may create an allocation of resources which has effects on the quality of life. It raises important issues concerning detrimental aspects of personal consumption versus collective consumption.

Pathways for enquiry

A survey of products

A survey of a small number of products which have

changed over time in response to consumer demand. How was the consumer preference expressed? Which producers responded? Was the new version of the product a commercial success?

A study of a consumer problem

A study of a consumer problem and how it was or was not put right.

A study of pressure group interaction with the media

A study of how one pressure group interacted with the media to change the balance of market power.

An investigation into the effects of changed consumer attitudes

An investigation of the economic effects of a change in consumers' attitudes to an environmental issue.

An investigation into the effects of the *Citizen's Charter*

An investigation of the effects of the *Citizen's Charter* on a particular public sector agency. Some local collaboration would be needed in order to do this.

Useful sources

➤ The Consumers Association, 2 Marylebone Road, London NW1 4DF
➤ Friends of the Earth has a publications catalogue: 26 Underwood Street, London N1 7JT. Tel: 0171-490 1555
➤ *Business Case Studies* by Ian Marcousé with David Lines (Longman, 2nd edn, 1994); 'A Pressure Group Triumph'.

Enquiry 4: What is the market power of stakeholders?

Stakeholders' powers have already been considered in Enquiry 3, when the interests of consumers and of society were examined. Here the focus is upon stakeholders within the business – the shareholders, the employees and the managers. The most

important aspects of the Enquiry concern the possibilities of conflicting interests creating issues which are difficult to resolve.

Synopsis

Students may be able to combine enquiry into the matter of pay increases, managerial pay, dividends and short-termism in the study of one firm. However, getting the information may not be easy.

The opening evidence gives a range of perspectives on the relative powers of different stakeholders, shareholders, employees and managers.

1 Stakeholders

The enquiry opens with a summary of the risks and rewards which may accrue to stakeholders, examining their respective vested interests.

2 Shareholders' powers

Measures of share performance are outlined. The relative importance of institutional shareholders as opposed to individuals is examined.

3 Employees' powers

This section focuses on the role of the trade unions and the changes which have taken place. It shows how union power has diminished and goes on to discuss the way in which recent trends in the labour market generally have changed many individuals' bargaining power. In particular, recent theories of human resource management have made employee friendly management practices much more prevalent. Lastly the legal framework of employee protection is examined.

4 Managers' interests

This is a brief review of leadership roles and the changing nature of management.

5 Conflicts and collaboration

The concluding section draws together a range of themes, showing how stakeholder interests may collide with each other. The important issue of employee involvement is addressed, as is that of the conflict between the need for flexible labour markets and the need for employee protection. Short-termism is touched on. It is pointed out that other conflicts of interest may arise in the future.

Pathways for enquiry

A local investigation

Local investigation has a part to play in this enquiry. Although it would be possible to look at a firm not previously investigated, it may be preferable to make this part of an ongoing enquiry linked to previous work.

Questions which may be addressed include:
➤ How many shareholders are there and what are their objectives?
➤ How have industrial relations developed in recent years?
➤ What provision is made for employee involvement?
➤ What type of contracts are given to employees?
➤ What changes have been made to the managerial structure?

Collecting information on conflicts of interest may be difficult. However, if the firm is already well known to students, it may be possible to read between the lines.

A trade union

Study of a trade union could cover:
➤ The objectives of primary importance to members
➤ The nature of industrial relations in the industry concerned
➤ The issues of paramount importance in recent negotiations
➤ Changes in the approach of trade unions in recent years
➤ An assessment of an individual's bargaining power at a particular point in time.

An evaluation of the pros and cons of a flexible labour force

Does increased flexibility reduce the market power of the employees? This issue seems likely to run for some time at the EU level.

Interviews with two managers

One interview should take place in a fairly hierarchical structure and the other in a flatter organisation. Find out to what extent each feels 'in control' of their situation. How do their responsibilities differ?

A study of manager/employee discrimination

Study a recent situation in which managers have been treated in one way and employees in another. The most obvious examples will occur in relation to their respective pay deals. What does this indicate about their relative market power?

Useful sources

Trade unions are often prepared to help. Many prepared statements for the recent House of Commons Select Committee investigations and are prepared to send these out. The TUC also has information available.

➤ Trade Union Congress, Congress House, Great Russell Street, London WC1B 3LS
➤ Data on pay is reported in *Labour Research*, the journal of the Labour Research Department. A subscription to this is £23.95, which, although too much for an individual centre, might be shared by two centres in the Nuffield network.
➤ The relative market power of men and women is dealt with in Brief 4, 'The War Between the Sexes', in The Economist Schools Briefs, *Labour Market Economics*, which appeared in 1994 and is available from Linda Denli, The Economist, 25 St. James's Street, London SW1A 1HG. These have other useful material on the labour market but are not really written from the standpoint of this option.
➤ *The Empty Raincoat* by Charles Handy (Hutchinson, 1994) although not directly relevant to questions of market power, makes many interesting points about flexible labour markets, and may prove useful in a general way. It was widely reported in the press at the time of publication and the articles may be accessible on CD-ROM.

Enquiry 5: What powers are applied by the government?

This enquiry considers the extent to which business is controlled by UK legislation and some of the reasons why governments have felt it necessary to intervene in the market.

Synopsis

1 The government and the market
Starting with a general overview of government activity, this section explores the change in the government's role which came with privatisation.

2 Regulation and deregulation
Consideration of the regulation which has been put in place as a result of privatisation is followed by examples of deregulation.

3 Legislation on monopoly and competition
The underlying philosophy of recent competition legislation is outlined, as are the procedures for referral of monopolies and restrictive practices to the MMC. The role of the EU is included along with a number of case studies.

4 Other means of control
In addition to controlling business by legislation, the government can persuade businesses to co-operate via a range of incentives and other devices. There is coverage of links between the private and public sectors, and the scope for using taxes and subsidies.

5 The power of the European Union
Through the Common Agriculture Policy and the measures to create a single market, the EU has considerable power to influence markets. In addition, much legislation covering business has its origins in Brussels rather than London.

Pathways for enquiry

The most fruitful line of enquiry may well be a recent event, investigation or debate which has been well covered in the press. This is also a good time for students to take an overview of the system and try to assess whether it is generally biased in favour of the consumer or the producer.

A regulatory body
Investigate recent pronouncements by a regulatory body such as OFTEL. What impact are the measures suggested by regulators likely to have which might benefit the consumer?

Monopolies and Mergers Commission
Investigate a recent ruling by the Monopolies and Mergers Commission.

The public sector
Gather information on the size and role of the public sector. How has it changed over the past decade? Has the market power of the government changed as a result?

A local business
Find out the impact of regulation on a local business. The main impact may come through product requirements or through constraints on employment conditions, or both. Would the firm welcome a move to reduce the amount of regulation? What are the reasons for its view?

Useful sources

The regulatory watchdog bodies are rather small organisations with limited scope for helping enquirers. However, their activities are well reported in the press and the best source of information will be CD-ROM.

➤ *The Blue Book* (HMSO) provides information on public expenditure and GDP.
➤ *Equity and Efficiency* by Margaret Wilkinson (Heinemann, 1993) provides detail on competition policy.
➤ *Economics Explained* by Peter Maunder et al. (Harper Collins, 3rd edn, 1995); Chapter 29 covers competition policy in detail.

Option 5: Business Strategies: How are decisions made?

Making correct decisions has always been regarded as *the* key skill in business because it separates the successful organisation from the unsuccessful. It is therefore hardly surprising that a whole industry, consisting of academics, managers and politicians has grown up, trying to determine the special ingredients to be found in making such decisions.

As in so many areas of life, the analysis of decision making goes through fashions. In the 1970s and into the 1980s, the notion of 'scientific decision making' prevailed. The philosophy behind this idea was that decisions could be broken down into their constituent parts and then analysed using scientific (by which was usually meant statistical) devices. The increasing ability of computers to deal with vast quantities of numerical data added credibility to this approach. It also coincided with the dominance of the Western 'mega-corporation' whose focus was arguably more on the market than on the role of individuals.

The problems with this 'scientific' approach were manifested as the 1980s moved into the rapidly changing world of the 1990s. There always had been those who disputed the enticing but ultimately spurious accuracy of computer generated predictions, but by this time there was also increasing evidence that successful organisations, usually run by the Japanese, were delegating more and more important decision making to lower and lower levels in their hierarchies – people who had no access to computers but whose knowledge of the way the company actually functioned was second to none.

The present state of affairs may appear slightly confusing but it is probably a fair compromise between using the undoubted power of numbers and contemporary number-crunching machines and the ability of the human mind to take all that information on board, and then add another, very special and unique ingredient. We may call that ingredient intuition, common sense, experience or whatever, but its existence marks out decision making not as a mechanical process but as an essentially human activity which is, as a result, utterly fascinating .

Teaching the option

Reference is made at the start of the book to management 'gurus' and the importance of their writing, but the work of Tom Peters and others demonstrates just how quickly thinking in the area of decision making can alter. In *Liberation Management* (Preface, page xxxi) Peters himself makes the point that his own work, from *In Search of Excellence* through *Thriving on Chaos* displays a history of error, or at least misconception, based on what he saw as the way successful organisations were run at the time. The pace of change – Peters refers to the 'Nanosecond Nineties' – is ever increasing and, inevitably, students reading *Business Strategies* will encounter opinions which will differ from those expressed therein.

This should be a cause for celebration, however. The absolute requirement when studying business decisions is to read, watch and listen: newspapers, the television, business people talking and so on, but to do all of it from a critical stance. *Business Strategies* will supply some technical tools, but the most important ones are intellectual and, perhaps surprisingly, emotional, because this book makes the point very clearly that intuition has as important a place in decision making as statistics.

Teaching this option, therefore, requires a judicious mix. On the one hand, there are some quite challenging numerical areas which will demand clear explanation, probably delivered in a structured way, and, in order to ensure learning in different contexts, plenty of practice exercises. On the other hand, students must enjoy the freedom to value their own opinions and emotional responses to problems, but within the kind of framework which the book supplies. The aim is that, by its end, they should be able to employ an array of intellectual and intuitive weapons to analyse problems critically.

It is the expectation of the Nuffield Project that students will, by this stage, have learned to work and investigate on their own. This option does require some secondary sources to enable personal research to take place. Access to newspaper articles is vital. CD-ROM should be available to all the students so that stories can be followed in a historical context. Any material thus accessed can be added to the student's portfolio.

At the same time, current newspaper material can be clipped and commentary made on its content. Regular features, such as 'My Biggest Mistake' which appeared in the *Independent on Sunday,* are clearly directly relevant to decision making.

In addition, however, a supply of serious management books is essential. It may be that the school or college library or its equivalent can be persuaded to stock single copies of such books, or it may be that the department itself can hold them for ease of student access. Whichever way is chosen, it is important that they are there and accessible. Most are very readable and contain case studies which can only enhance the students' interest and enthusiasm for the subject.

Other rich sources of case studies are books written for the GNVQ or A Level business studies market. Probably the best known of these is *Business Case Studies* by Ian Marcousé with David Lines (Longman, 2nd edn, 1994). The cases are categorised into concept areas for ease of reference

and a *Teacher's Guide,* containing answers, is also available. The book includes specific cases taking decision making as a theme, including two which also cover particular areas in *Business Strategies*: Number 8 which involves using decision trees and Number 9, weighted averages.

Another of Ian Marcousé's books, *Business Calculations and Statistics* (Longman, 1994), is useful for some of the numerical concepts, placed within a business context. It contains plenty of exercises which are useful practice in ensuring that the material is thoroughly learnt and understood.

The introduction to *Business Strategies* contains a list of possible reading and the sources of the quotes from the opening evidence at the beginning of each enquiry are also ones which might be acquired over time. In addition, there are many others which would be of value and they are detailed below under the heading 'useful sources'. Many of these are priced below, or only slightly above, the £10 level. Most of them are not the kind of books which find their way into the brochures of educational publishers, so an annual pilgrimage to a local retailer could be very fruitful.

There are also many useful, and very often free, publications. For instance the Department for Employment will send their magazine *Employment News* to centres; it contains articles about the way legislation may impinge upon business decisions. Likewise, the CBI, the TUC and the Office of Fair Trading also produce material which is relevant. Should an important piece of legislation be passed during the A Level course, it might be possible to role play a scenario-planning meeting where different effects of the legislation were brainstormed. Groups of students could take the parts of different interest groups and having magazine articles to inform the discussion would then be invaluable.

Other magazines are, regrettably, not free. One thinks of *Management Today* and even *The Harvard Business Review.* As they would have clear relevance to the whole of the course, however, it might be considered a reasonable investment to purchase subscriptions.

There are also magazines which are aimed more at the student market, such as *Business Studies* published by Anforme Ltd, Prudhoe, Northumberland and *The Business Studies Review* published by Philip Allen Ltd, Oxford. They contain directly relevant and highly readable articles which can very often provide a springboard for debate and discussion.

The use of IT in decision making is highly recommended. *Beat the Boss,* published by Ronald Brech, creates a business environment which encourages decision taking which is both statistical and intuitive, and which also encourages students to look at firms operating within a macroenvironment as well as within their own markets.

UNISIM, published by Unilever, is similar to *Beat the Boss* in that it involves making important decisions within a team handling a large number of variables. The use of both *Beat the Boss* and UNISIM within the context of this option is rather different from the way they might be used elsewhere, however. It is certainly important to analyse what to do next, but more important to analyse how the decisions were arrived at. It is quite possible that students could observe how these processes changed as they work their way through the investigations in *Business Strategies*.

The Nuffield *Data Book*, and the Investigations and Data disk supplied by Statistics for Education, 5 Bridge Street, Bishop's Stortford, Herts CM23 2JU, are essential. Real world data will supply material that can be processed in the ways described in the book, for example by calculating measures of dispersion. Needless to say, care must be taken when the machine carries out complicated tasks, such as working out the standard deviation, that the students are aware of the actual processes that are involved.

Clearly, in a book which has decision making as its focus, there is a need to involve the local business community in some way or other in order to analyse how decisions are actually made. This is where the local Training and Enterprise Council (TEC) should be useful, as well as Chambers of Commerce, Rotary and Lion's Clubs (helpful involvement in fund raising often carries a *quid pro quo* with such bodies), and so on.

Contact with business may take the apparently rather mundane form of interviews carried out by students; mundane but nevertheless useful if the interviews are carefully structured. On the other hand, it may be better to get local businesspeople to come in to talk to the students about the way they make decisions because the students will feel less intimidated. The questions must still be carefully rehearsed to avoid painful and embarrassing silences. The use of businesses is further developed as an alternative pathway to Enquiry 5, below.

Educational research shows that the best and most effective learning takes place when students relate what they learn in the classroom to what is going on in their own lives. They, like everyone else, make thousands of decisions every day and, while the thrust of the book is clearly focused on business decisions, there is no harm, and indeed positive benefit, in referring back to apparently prosaic decisions and asking if they could be structured in the way the book suggests. This is hardly a revolutionary pedagogy, of course, but perhaps it is one which is particularly relevant and effective with this option.

Enquiry 1: How does decision making begin?

The opening enquiry sets the tone for the whole book, i.e. information is essential but it must be treated with care. Data need to be structured and processed to be effective but can cloud issues rather than clarifying them unless treated with respect and some caution. The human aspect of decision making is emphasised throughout.

Synopsis

1 Analysing the problem to gain an advantage

The enquiry opens by introducing the concept of issues diagrams. These diagrams are designed to break down major problems into their component parts, so that they become less daunting and therefore more soluble. This promotes the idea of asking the right question to find the solution that is being sought, but that does not imply being hamstrung by such a systematic approach. Instead, it should promote creative and imaginative thinking to find solutions. Only by such a creative process can a firm stay ahead of the competition. Of course, part of remaining competitive is trying to second-guess what the market will demand, and what others will produce. Hence, the notions of strategic axes of freedom are introduced as an aid to suggest a way forward.

2 Gathering information

The value of information in a business context is self-evident but gathering and processing such information is complicated and costly. Information technology can overcome both of these disadvantages and provides a powerful tool with which to meet the challenges of the market place. Getting close to customers is increasingly vital, given an ever faster rate of change, and that often means sharing information rather than jealously guarding it until product launch. IBM is used as a case study of how a company has moved from product to market orientation by sharing plans rather than assuming that it knows best. Finally, the section ends on a lighter note by examining gossip and the role it plays in the information stream within an organisation.

3 Processing information

This section uses a case study of Newtown College to demonstrate how the acquisition of information can become almost an aim in itself. Unless that information is processed properly, by making sure the right people get the data in the right form, the whole exercise can prove to be an expensive waste, leading to incorrect decision making. One way to process information is often to summarise it using the basic statistical techniques of averages and standard deviation.

4 Extracting the information from the data

Sometimes data in their raw state simply obscure the information which they contain. Index numbers can help to disentangle the numbers so that they can be compared and analysed more quickly and simply. Once again, the strength of IT is demonstrated through electronic shopping, which not only helps consumers, but also enables producers to keep a close watch on their stock, the items which are most in demand, and those which are fading.

Pathways for enquiry

Averages and standard deviation

The students should be quite familiar with the Nuffield Data disk by this stage. Given the wealth of real-world statistics which it contains, it is a rich source of material for learning about averages and standard deviations. The computer will carry out these calculations effortlessly, of course, but it might be an idea to insist that students work them out manually and then to check their results against the ones generated by the machine. One example might be to use the data disk to investigate sales of singles, LPs, cassettes and CDs over the past 15 years. Students could analyse their findings using, firstly, the raw data, and then indices. Then, over two five-year periods, they could compare mean sales and standard deviations for each of the products. It would obviously be important to think about which two periods to choose. For instance, it might be instructive to compare a period of boom like the late 1980s with a period of slump such as the early 1990s. The obvious questions which this would raise would be: 'What does this information tell you about each of the markets, and what does it tell you about the record industry as a whole?'

A structured approach to decision making

One of the key points about the decision-making process which is stated in *Business Strategies* is that a structured approach can often clarify thinking in a way that makes the decision easier to handle. For example, students might be asked to select a problem that faces them in studying for A Levels. They will probably feel they haven't enough money to pay for their social lives, clothes, CDs or whatever. They should set down the question: 'How can my income match what I want (social life/clothes/CDs, etc.)?', and then break down that question into smaller ones, perhaps starting from such as, 'How can I decrease my costs?' and, 'How can I increase my income?'. Then extend the lines from those into more and more detailed ones. Once that is done, it is vital to stress that their thinking must be creative in order to suggest new solutions.

A critique

Often one of the most challenging things which teachers of A level have to face is persuading students to read beyond the immediately available books. It may not be so difficult in the case of those written by Tom Peters. An interesting section in Peters's book *Liberation Management* lies on pages 107–127. It concerns the IT revolution and the way it is affecting all our lives. It is a fascinating, glimpse into the future. As an interesting academic exercise combining a number of skills, ask students to write a précis of its contents. This should take the form of a memo to the senior management of a firm producing traditional engineering products which it sells to industry (or any other scenario which you may prefer). The finished copy must be, at the most, one and a half pages long, plus half a page of criticism and evaluation.

Turning a hobby into a job

A lot of people would like to turn their hobby into a job. If there are students who are thinking along those lines, turn it into an opening question and ask them to brainstorm answers. They should go into the community to interview people who have achieved this ambition and find out what it is like; in what ways does it affect their decision making and is the job still a hobby now it is a job! The local golf professional is probably one of these people, or the owner of/worker in a gardening centre. The local sports centre is probably managed by one, and car dealers are often people who have a tremendous enthusiasm for the product they sell. At the end of the exercise the students must

organise the data collected and draw valid and evaluated conclusions.

Useful sources

➤ *Liberation Management* by T. Peters (Macmillan, 1992); pages 107–127.
➤ *How to get ahead in Business* ed. by T. Cannon (Virgin Books, 1993); Chapter 12. This is an entertaining book which is both cheap and easy to read. It even comes in what might be termed 'word bites' – ideal for today's brought-up-on-TV youth!

Enquiry 2: What is to be decided?

Part of any structured decision making is deciding what is to be achieved – in other words the aims and objectives. Beyond that there are different kinds of decisions which are relevant to different situations, and they must be applied appropriately, particularly when the actions of competitors are taken into account.

Synopsis

1 Deciding what to do – aims, objectives and strategies

This section builds upon work which was encountered in the stages, especially Units 2/1 and 4/3. It relates to the experiences which students have when they think about their potential career paths; the relationships between different levels of objectives: primary and secondary; and the strategies which can be employed to achieve those goals.

2 Management by objectives

Looking at management by objectives in a current context, it is important that the whole philosophy be examined in a critical way. Obviously, conflicting objectives must be avoided, but the work of writers such as Peters suggests that people must be allowed to operate within a broader framework – one related to the entire image of the organisation. Ford's vision of its role as a company is considered critically in this context.

3 Different kinds of decisions

Programmed and non-programmed decisions are examined in this section. The former are those which occur almost without thought – the firm has laid down clear guidelines and the employee follows them. Non-programmed decisions require employees to break new ground and take responsibility for their actions. They also tend to commit the company more, and this leads on to the distinction between tactical and strategic decisions. Strategic decisions are the ones which carry the very highest level of risk. Partly because of the risk element and partly because they usually involve the entire operation of the company, they are very often taken at the very highest level, usually by the board of directors.

4 Decision making and competition

Long-run strategies to beat the competition often involve short-term tactics. This section offers a fictitious case study to show how market domination in the long term can be achieved through following a strategic path. Finally, a distinction is drawn between logistic and management processes in what Ansoff calls 'goal-seeking organisations'. The former are concerned with taking resources from the environment and producing goods and services, which are then offered back into the environment, while the latter handles information in three decision areas: strategic, administrative and operational.

Pathways for enquiry

Company mission statements

In groups, send away for the mission statements of five major companies, asking at the same time how they go about meeting them. While waiting for the replies, interview five business people about their aims. Some may be completely vague, while others may say 'to make a profit' or 'to survive', in which case ask them to be more specific. In either case, try to discover how they achieve their aims, however unclear. Present your results to the rest of the class.

Student decision making

In order to relate what the students are studying in their classrooms to the theory, get them to think in detail about the decisions they make during a normal day at college. They should then write down a selection and divide them up into strategic and tactical, programmed and non-programmed. A degree of sensitivity may be involved here! It may be that, in order to complete this exercise, students will have to articulate their own aims and objectives. This might be too personal but, if it is, it can be de-personalised by discussing whether it is a good thing to have clearly thought-through life aims and objectives. Such a discussion can easily and fruitfully be related to the business environment.

Appraising advertisements

Set students the following task: go through newspapers and magazines and look at the advertisements in a critical way to see what they are saying about the *company*, as much as the product. Some advertisements are actually generic, that is to say, they are not actually trying to sell particular products at all; they are all about projecting an image. Analyse these in particular. Why are the companies advertising like this? Is something happening in their market which is causing them to act in this way?

Business case studies

There are seven cases relating to decision making in *Business Case Studies*. In particular, Numbers 4, 8 and 9 relate to marketing and competition.

Useful sources

➤ *Liberation Management* by T. Peters (Macmillan, 1992); pages 42–43; 757–760.
➤ *Business Management* by R. Erskin (Prentice Hall, 1991); Chapters 8 and 10 especially. Overall, an interesting and challenging text written for undergraduates but quite accessible to good sixth formers.

Enquiry 3: How can communication aid decision making?

This enquiry focuses on the people involved in decisions. Managers spend a lot of their time making decisions; this is important, but so, too, is the way they motivate people. That may depend on the style of leadership used. Today employees are also recognised as vital elements in the decision-making process and so participation schemes which are genuinely designed to involve them are vital. The way the company itself is organised may help or hinder decision making, but having a well-established way of doing things is not necessarily an automatic recipe for success.

Synopsis

1 Decision making in groups

The enquiry opens by emphasising the distinction between simply listening to employees' opinions and drawing them fully into the decision making process, which is genuine employee participation. Central to this principle is the way that opinions can be expressed in groups, exploiting the strengths of team-work. This leads into a discussion of the entire process of Japanisation and the use of quality circles. Nevertheless, not all groups work together effectively as teams, and that is an important notion which also requires investigation.

2 Management styles and decision making

This section draws a distinction between managing the task and managing the human side of the activity. This naturally leads into different leadership styles, from the democratic through to the autocratic, developing, in turn, to the important notion of appropriateness – the right style for the prevailing situation, here called the pendulum approach.

3 Company structures and decision making

The way the company is structured has a considerable influence over how effective communication within it is. Large organisations are notorious for not responding to new and creative ideas, whereas in a business world of constantly increasing rates of change, a positive response is absolutely vital. At the same time it is not always advantageous to be small – Tom Peters suggests that

the next generation of companies will have to 'think big and act small'. Certainly, company structures will have to be designed to allow people room; in other words to *enable* people to exploit their full potential.

4 Chaos and conflict

This section offers an alternative view of consensus, saying that it is not necessarily a good thing. Sometimes being forced to argue a position strengthens the decision-making process. A similar situation prevails when companies get into a particular 'mindset' – a way of doing things that has gone on for so long that the personnel begin to think that their way is the only way. In such a situation, turmoil can provoke a complete turn-round of the company's fortunes.

Pathways for enquiry

A company visit

You may have a Japanese-owned company in your locality. Ask if you can visit the factory to talk to the personnel department (it may be called by another name) about employee participation schemes and the way management relates to the workforce. Do the same with a UK firm and make a comparison. Ask both about the process of decision making. Is it top down or bottom up? How are decisions transmitted? How quickly can changes be made? What is the role of employee organisations within the firm? How is the company organised in terms of its hierarchy? Ask for a diagram of the structure. There are many more questions which can be thought up before the visit. It is, however, important to stress to the firm that, as a group, you will wish to ask questions of people and not just have a factory visit, although that, too, will undoubtedly be interesting. For the more ambitious, similar trips can be arranged with firms in other EU countries (a useful source of help in arranging such visits is *European Awareness 14–18*, available from TEED National Distribution Centre, PO Box 12, West PDO, Leen Gate, Nottingham NG7 2GB).

Organisation and leadership in the armed forces

Invite an officer from any of the armed forces to come to

your college to talk about organisation and leadership. The services often see a recruiting advantage to be gained from such visits and are therefore eager to speak to students. Explain clearly what you want from them and you will probably get a very professional presentation and some considerable surprises!

Leadership in a business organisation

Business Case Studies offers no fewer than 11 under the leadership heading, including Number 73, which covers a number of areas relevant to production, morale and organisation.

An organisation chart

An interesting but sometimes politically delicate exercise is to ask students to construct a diagram of the organisational structure of their own school or college. It is up to individual teachers whether this is practical or not. The most common hierarchy is quite conventional, although also often quite progressive in that spans of control can be wide. The lines of communication are, however, rather opaque, especially where the academic and pastoral sides are considered. A lively discussion can often ensue after examining the hierarchy, especially if students are asked to role-play management consultants presenting their findings to the head or principal.

Advantage/disadvantages of office/home work

Write to the *Los Angeles Times* and/or look up on CD-ROM the impact of the 1993 earthquake on the changes in working habits of people in and around the conurbation, which were caused by the devastation of conventional communication links. Relate data from these sources to surveys of home working in the UK. What are the implications for organisations, and for employees, of increasing numbers of people working from home?

Useful sources

➤ *Liberation Management* by T. Peters (Macmillan, 1992); pages 42–43; 757–760
➤ *Funny Business* by J-L. Barsoux (Cassell, 1993); pages 103-106. The book takes a light-hearted

but serious look at the way business operates. It also has cartoons and should appeal to the average sixth former.
➤ *Business Management* by R. Erskin (Prentice Hall, 1991); Chapter 9.
➤ *Management Teams: Why they Succeed or Fail* by R. M. Belbin (Butterworth, Heinemann, 1981)
➤ *Head to Head: The Coming Economic Battle among Japan, Europe and America* by L. Thurow (Nicholas Brealey, 1993). The original book caused a storm in the USA when it was first published, as it appeared to suggest the terminal decline of American industry in the face of an inexorable advance by Japan. This version takes a critical look at the European Union's potential in the world's economy, related to the other big players. Not a book for the faint hearted but plenty of food for thought.
➤ *The Workplace Revolution* by C. C. Cooper and S. Lewis (Kogan Page, 1993).

Enquiry 4: How can outcomes be analysed?

This Enquiry pulls together much of the numerical work found within the book. That said, as it progresses it moves towards an increasing emphasis on the shortcomings of relying on numbers too much. There are techniques that have to be learnt, especially as they can only be criticised effectively from a position of knowledge and not ignorance, but it is the idea of balanced decision making which is emphasised in the end.

Synopsis

1 Dealing with risk

The enquiry opens with a very short section introducing the notion of probability and the extreme values of zero and one.

2 Choosing between alternatives: decision trees

A decision tree is built up, based upon a sixth former's career choices, including the possibilities of particular salary levels. These expected values are then used with probabilities in order to aid the final decision but it is stressed that the numerical side is only one aspect of the decision and that non-quantitative factors are also important.

If more detail is needed on decision trees, turn to Chapter 8, *Business Calculations and Statistics* by Ian Marcousé (Longman, 1994).

3 Investment appraisal

This section goes through average rate of return, discounted cash flow, present value, net present value and internal rate of return as a way of helping businesses with their investment decisions. The calculations are developed around a case study.

4 Predicting the future

Scenario planning is introduced as a new way for firms to examine alternatives. A number of scenarios are brainstormed and then the likelihood of each occurring is analysed. An emphasis is placed on the elements, both within and outside the firm, which might impact upon the decision in the future, in particular competition, and the economic, political, technical, social and demographic environment. There is a brief section on moving averages, building on what has been done in Unit 4/1. Here they are mentioned as a warning to those who overvalue their usefulness as a way of predicting the future.

5 New methods of decision making

In a way, there has been something of a backlash against decision making based largely on figures. Numbers tend to give a spurious impression of accuracy, especially when projected forward. On the other hand, it is relatively easy to look at a number of options and then rank them on a preference scale. Having done that, it is important not only to look at the alternatives, but also to weight them according to their perceived importance. Numerical data can then be introduced, but on a relative scale. The choice of a company car is the case study used to demonstrate this, looking at the criteria of cost and benefit – here

taken to be the brand of car. These are weighted, with cost being given a much higher emphasis than brand.

Pathways for enquiry

Uses and limitations of data

Business Case Studies contains three cases which are excellent exercises on the uses and limitations of data. Number 37 is an amusing one on the advantages of deductive reasoning in decision trees employed by Sherlock Holmes; Number 42 extends the concept to include SWOT analysis and a critique of the technique's usefulness; and Number 79 also includes extrapolating time series data. Investment appraisal is dealt with in Cases 12 and 16 in particular. Working through the questions will, of course, also provide useful revision for the stages as well as exploring the concepts at issue in this option.

Scenario planning

Clearly, what happens in the immediate and longer-term future is something of considerable importance to young people who are at a stage when they are thinking about serious life issues such as careers, higher education, personal relationships and so on. Arrange the students into groups and get each group to come up with alternative scenarios for the next five, ten or 20 years (or whatever is appropriate). The limit of the scenario can be specified: the social, political, business or physical environments are obvious candidates. The scenarios should be brainstormed but built around the best case, most likely case and worst case alternatives.

Discounting tables

It is important that students are familiar with discounting tables because they lead to a deeper understanding of DCF and IRR. Tables are often found at the back of finance and accounting texts, but an excellent source for the course in general, and one which also contains tables, is David Myddleton's *Accounting and Financial Decisions* (Longman, 1991). Simple exercises, with amounts being discounted back to present values, are usually sufficient, but the starting point must be the notion of the *time value of money*, which lies at the heart of all financial discounting.

Internal rates of return graph

Drawing an internal rates of return graph can be difficult, but it is necessary to do this in order to relate IRR to DCF. In fact, taking three or four points on the graph usually supplies enough information to get quite close to the ideal. The first point is quite straightforward: when the discount rate is zero the DCF value is the total sum of the inflows. Next plot the figures for rates of 5%, 10% and 15%. To save time, this can be done in groups, or more quickly still by using a computer spreadsheet. Then ask them to plot the result and read off the discount rate which will yield a value of zero for the project. Using a computer spreadsheet offers a major advantage in that the package will also plot the graph, but if the students don't know already, don't tell them until after they have done it manually!

Useful sources

➤ *How to get ahead in business* by T. Cannon (Virgin Books, 1993); Chapter 6.

Enquiry 5: What are the constraints on decision making?

It is clear that no decision can be taken in isolation. If there were no opportunity cost then there would *be* no decision! As far as businesses are concerned, the limits to action are determined by factors either within or outside the organisation, and the importance of each will depend on the type of decision and the resources which are available.

Synopsis

1 Constraints on decision making

Just as an individual is constrained by opportunity cost, so too are businesses. This section looks at the internal constraints which influence firms, concentrating on shareholder power. There is a brief debate over whether shareholders in the UK are too concerned with short-term gains, as opposed to the Japanese system of *keiretsu*, where linked groups have shares in each other and therefore have an interest in maintaining each other over the medium to long term. The debate then moves to the role of trade unions and their place within the legal framework as it currently exists.

2 External constraints

This section opens the debate on whether the law acts as a constraint or whether it provides a 'level playing field' which makes things fair for all sides. Equal opportunities legislation is examined in some depth, looking at the role of women in the workforce. This moves on to the general political and economic environment within which businesses operate, including an examination of the assumption that all businesses prefer low-spending, low-taxation governments. Finally, the environment as a constraint, but also as a business opportunity, is examined.

3 Should the major constraint on decision making be financial?

This section questions the all too frequently made assumption that cost cuts must always be made in order to increase profitability. A case study of a pub demonstrates that, in certain cases, cutting costs too far hurts revenue even more, so that, in the end, profitability actually falls. This leads naturally into value analysis which starts from the premise that the product must not in any sense appear inferior in the consumers' eyes, but still be produced at the lowest cost possible.

4 Quality as a criterion for decision making

Quality is a current 'buzz word' in business and this section introduces quality circles and TQM (total quality management), using writers such as Tom Peters to demonstrate how vital quality is today. BS 5750 is described as a way of raising quality standards but it is also questioned as being little more than a way of continuing the status quo. A critical look at Japanese methods should indicate that there is no final answer in business studies. Indeed, the book ends with a degree of introspection, by evaluating the messages which it has been putting across. For instance, it looks at constraints which sometimes turn into opportunities; it looks at decision making which is, on the one hand, systematic, and numerical, and, on the other, intuitive. The final case study brings these elements together to show how these apparent contradictions are not, in fact, that way at all. By this stage, the students should be able to examine the decision-making process and, indeed, the decision itself, in a way that would have been quite impossible before starting the option.

Pathways for enquiry

Shareholder power

On CD-ROM, look up instances of shareholder power being exercised in the past two years. Then write (ideally on a word processor) to the companies concerned (using your home rather than school or college address). Say that you are considering buying their shares but, before doing so, you are trying to find out about their policy towards environmental issues or whatever they were previously in the news for. Has their policy or attitude changed?

Equal opportunities policies

Write to a number of local and national firms about their policies on equal opportunities legislation. Ask specific questions: what proportion of your workforce are women/disabled/from ethnic minorities? Alternatively, invite people from business into the college and ask the same questions, or go to the businesses themselves and ask. Don't restrict yourself to profit-maximising organisations either. Local government, the police and the National Health Service are huge employers. Find out their policies – both in theory and in practice. Contact national organisations promoting the interests of minorities and ask about progress, or the lack of it in integrating their members into the business community. Don't just collect the data, analyse it. Compare the types of organisations and the goods or services they produce. Relate where they work to the ethnic mix in that locality. Use the Nuffield regional network if such data are not readily available elsewhere.

Design and value analysis

Invite a member of the technology department in your school or college to talk to the students about good design and value analysis. Ask the person to bring along examples if possible. The different perspective from another discipline is fascinating but make sure that students ask questions about design from the economics/business perspective with which, by now, they should be quite familiar.

Focus on the real world

The end of the option is clearly the time to bring all the elements of the decision-making process to bear. This is where the involvement of local businesspeople is vital. One option, as suggested in the introduction, is to have students go to organisations and ask how a particular decision, or set of decisions, was or were arrived at. It is important to focus on a real-world situation and this may be better achieved by asking the person to come into school or college because then the session can be more structured. A far more ambitious plan would be to organise a conference, perhaps involving other Nuffield centres in the locality, using decision making as a theme. The task would be to find someone willing to come in and present a scenario of what happened to them up to the point of making a crucial decision.

The students could then go away in groups and discuss what *they* would do next if they had been in the position of having to decide. After a plenary session discussing everyone's ideas, the real-life 'solution' could be given, although one would have to point out that what was actually done in real life does not always correspond to an optimum. If that is the case, of course, the students would have learned another invaluable lesson. Finding people willing to bare their souls in this way may not appear to be very easy but, very often, someone who has subsequently been highly successful is prepared to come in and discuss a situation where he or she made a bad decision as well as good ones, and the reasons that led up to it. Parents of students on the course are often a rich source in this regard, but the local Training and Enterprise Council (TEC) should also be able to help.

Useful sources

➤ *The Seamless Enterprise* by D. Dimancescu (Harper Collins, 1992). Essentially about TQM and the way it can be incorporated into the entire organisation.

Option 6: Corporate Responsibility: Is business accountable?

The open-ended and slightly ambiguous quality about this option title is intentional. Perhaps the first supplementary question to arise is, 'accountable to whom – or what?' Who or what, indeed, is 'business'? And on what principles or evidence would accountability rest? The agenda is intriguing, full of possibilities and with great scope for originality.

As the rather functional listing in the syllabus indicates, this option directs enquiry towards the nature of the joint stock company, the relationship between shareholders, directors, managers and employees – and the responsibilities of the firm towards its other stakeholders: creditors, suppliers, customers, communities and subsidiaries abroad. The range of enquiry also moves outwards to consider wider questions of environmental, cultural and ethical responsibility.

The subject of business accountability has always been contentious. Debate was often polarised between those who fundamentally believed or disbelieved in the principle of private, profit-led enterprise. The privatisation programmes since the 1980s and the worldwide collapse of state communism have significantly altered this perspective. If the business corporation is to be the normal model in organising production, then it is clear that it also carries enormous responsibilities. Arguably, a new need exists to ensure that market forces are benign in their effect, not just for traditional beneficiaries such as shareholders, but for interest groups throughout society. As a philosophy, popular capitalism depends on popularity.

Despite this background, the territory that students are being asked to explore in this option is actually quite seldom explored. The very concept of stakeholders did not gain currency in

Britain until the early 1990s and is still sketchily covered in most textbooks. The media tend to show rather sporadic bursts of interest in the issues of accountability, according to the currency of specific news stories. Higher education has shown a more consistent pattern of increased commitment and many business schools now give accountability problems serious and sustained attention. It certainly seems that the theme is in a period of rapid development and is likely to remain a major focus for debate and research.

Teaching the option

It is important for students to understand the terms of reference as quickly as possible and to move inside the 'field' of the option theme. Fortunately, this is well populated with stories that carry a strong human appeal. Indeed a high-profile case study (e.g. Maxwell Communications or the *Exxon Valdez* oil spill) may be an effective way to introduce the option. Ultimately, of course, all the enquiries lead towards some fairly abstract – and sometimes philosophical – issues. However, it will probably be best for these to emerge through the work and for the initial teaching focus to be more concrete. In the same way, some historical perspective will be very valuable but it is likely to be best learnt through case examples taken from an earlier period.

Useful sources for research are recommended for each enquiry. Mainstream texts tend to be rather thin in their coverage but there is a fast-growing literature aimed at higher and professional education and at business managers. Selectivity is important here but short extracts and case examples should be very useful. Companies themselves are obviously another key source. The large public companies are usually helpful in supplying annual reports and other published material, but obtaining answers to specific questions is often much more difficult. Private companies are very variable but, once they agree to co-operate, can be the best source of all. A particular difficulty with all company contacts is communicating the exact nature of the enquiry. Students will need help in this respect. Large firms are very prone to sending out the same glossy PR for all 'school projects', while small companies may find the line of enquiry unfamiliar or feel worried about the implications for confidentiality. These problems can all be overcome but tact and persistence are often necessary. Government agencies and quangos, as well as pressure groups, can be very helpful. There are many suggestions in this guide but the possibilities are endless and students should be as enterprising as they can.

Enquiry 1: What is business responsibility?

The enquiry opens by considering the origin and history of business responsibility. The ideas of entrepreneurship and ownership are then surveyed. This leads into analysis of the classic market model and the human realities of shifts in competitive advantage. The claims of external, as opposed to internal, stakeholders are examined, together with minimum and maximum interpretations of accountability to stakeholders. The final section deals with the significance of ethical responsibility.

Synopsis

The opening evidence aims to illustrate the extremely diverse and conflicting views of business responsibility. It intentionally touches on the classic debate over the means and ends of capitalism, while introducing a historical perspective.

1 Business and responsibility
The fundamental nature and importance of business activity is reaffirmed. The idea of the entrepreneur

is shown to be inseparable from interaction with society: thus the basic notion of stakeholders emerges. The *laissez-faire* model of private business ownership is illustrated in the context of the Industrial Revolution, with contrasting reference to Robert Owen's experiments at New Lanark. These then introduce the great Victorian business philanthropists and their class-based ideas of moral and social improvement.

2 Who is in charge?
The section begins with the concept of the sole trader and partnership with unlimited liability. The significance of incorporation and limited liability is carried through into consideration of the roles of shareholders and directors. The importance of loan capital is addressed. Growth of an enterprise then highlights the potential split between ownership and control. Public companies and the Stock Exchange raise the issue of shareholders who play no part in the management or decision-making process. Institutional investors are introduced, with some assessment of City opinion. The section ends by raising the basic question: 'Who actually holds authority within a large quoted company?'

3 Answering to the market
The opener here is Adam Smith's 'invisible hand' and the *laissez-faire* ideal of self-optimising systems. The idea of markets working in a 'virtuous circle' is linked to the model of perfect competition. The parallel importance of the public sector in most Western countries is stressed. In the battleground of market forces, comparison is made between the social losers and communities well placed to gain.

4 Claims outside the market
The nature of claims beyond the strict jurisdiction of market forces is placed in the context of the spectrum within which business responsibility can be interpreted. The emerging case for a maximum interpretation of business responsibility is explained through the formal stakeholder model. This is contrasted with the 'purist' position of

direct profit maximisation and personal reward for adept response to market forces. The polarisation of interpretations is expressed through statements from Milton Friedman and Anita Roddick. Finally, it is suggested that corporate culture is a vital determinant in how far firms acknowledge the claims of different stakeholders.

5 Business ethics

The nature and diversity of ethical problems in business is introduced. The rising profile of the subject during the 1990s is stressed. A distinction is made between explicit and implicit ethical decisions. All strategic business decisions involve some ethical content and every firm must accept ethical trade-offs. Some large firms have introduced 'ethical codes' to assist their managers. A reputation for ethical behaviour may actually increase the value of a firm and its brands – with the converse equally true. In any case, corporate self-regulation helps to make government intervention less likely.

Pathways for enquiry

Development of business responsibility in an organisation

Students could research the historical development of business responsibility in any *one* enterprise. A family business – national or local – might be particularly interesting. Descriptive evidence (e.g. from company publicity or externally written history/biography) would be useful but there should also be analysis of how the acknowledgement of responsibility has changed and why.

A survey of business aims

A small survey of business aims could collect evidence and then analyse similarities and differences between firms. Assessment could be made of how far aims were real and whether any 'hidden agendas' existed. The survey could be nationally or locally based.

An investigation into the rights of owners and shareholders

The rights of owners and shareholders could be researched and probed. Perhaps two local business owners could be interviewed to explore their perception of the rights carried by ownership. Do these rights carry any responsibilities? Then a short survey of shareholders in national companies (parents, friends, staff, etc.) could make parallel enquiries. Finally, the two sets of responses could be contrasted and evaluated.

Winners and losers

This is a study of winners and losers. Business closure/development/expansion is probably the best theme and has the advantage of being readily accessible to research. Examples could include a local business closure or launch; a relocation decision; development of a supermarket, shopping centre, business park or industrial estate; a project related to leisure and tourism. The aim would be to identify the winners and the losers that arise from the decision concerned. Official stress will obviously be on winners: the student should find the losers too. The setting will probably be local but a national, or even international, example is perfectly possible given adequate research material.

Shareholder representation

The aim here is to show how any stakeholder may assert a stronger claim for representation in a firm's decision process. It is important that some fairly specific change in the status quo is explored. This might be the action of a trade union or some dismissed workers. It might feature the activities of shareholders or of a pressure group. It could look at a new environmental awareness or the demands of a community upon a firm. In each case, the emphasis should be on the nature of the claim, the method of its advancement and the response of the firm.

Business responsibility

The issue of business responsibility could be debated in class. This could work well as a formal debate or as a simulated debate between 'Anita Roddick' and 'Milton Friedman' plus their supporters. All students would need to make careful preparations, planning both arguments and counter-arguments.

Useful sources

➤ *Business Responsibility* by Tom Cannon (Pitman, 1992) is very expensive (£30) but very useful indeed.

➤ *Business and Society* by Edmund Marshall (Routledge, 1993) is recommended for the teacher.

➤ *Changing Corporate Values* by Richard Adams et al. (Kogan Page, 1991) is practical and useful for the whole option.

➤ Able students may even want to look at something more philosophical such as *A History of Economic Thought* by William Barber (Pelican, 1967).

➤ *Capitalism and Freedom* by Milton Friedman (University of Chicago Press, 1962) could be read as selected extracts.

➤ *Body and Soul* by Anita Roddick (Ebury Press, 1992) is very readable for students.

➤ *An Introduction to Business Ethics* by G. D. Chryssides and J. H. Kaler (Chapman & Hall, 1993) is very comprehensive, with useful readings and case studies but is difficult for students.

➤ The History Department should be useful and something can be gleaned from most texts on social and economic history even if they seem off-putting at first!

➤ Company reports are useful, as ever.

➤ National press commentary is quite frequent and relevant issues in local papers are very valuable.

Enquiry 2: What do firms disclose?

In one sense this enquiry is a research project into the present state of corporate disclosure. However, what firms disclose explicitly is only a starting point. Much of the reality is hidden under the stream of rather bland information that is issued by companies or the earnest statements of goodwill for stakeholders. Some of this official information will be penetrated in Enquiries 3 and 4, but this is the opportunity to reach inside firms' statutory and voluntary disclosure, carrying out the analysis and making the deductions that are possible.

It is important that students become thoroughly familiar with the handling and simple interpretation of a company annual report and accounts. They should all have enough practice to be confident in identifying the important sections and in extracting and analysing the key data.

Synopsis

1 The directors' dilemma

This section introduces the enquiry with the legitimate needs of stakeholders for information from any firm. It points out the counteractive wish of firms for confidentiality which must be set against the regulatory, social and ethical arguments for disclosure. The legal requirements for companies to supply information are briefly outlined.

2 The Annual Report and Accounts

A fairly detailed explanation of a typical report is provided. Examples are taken from a range of major companies. Coverage of the financial statements is only descriptive in this section. The main aim is to help students to find their way around an up-to-date company report.

3 The published accounts explained

The basic purpose of financial accounts is outlined, with an introduction to the key accounting concepts. Recent changes in reporting regulations are covered, including the work of the relatively new Accounting Standards Board. The profit and loss account and the balance sheet are then explained in some detail (using Tate & Lyle plc as an example) with a brief outline of the cash flow statement and the other accounting statements.

4 Evaluating accounts

The first part deals with ratio analysis and its applications. Some important ratios are defined. The problem of inflation is then addressed, with examples of how the distinction between current and constant year values affects reported results. A discussion of window dressing follows, with an explanation of some common techniques.

5 Other sources of disclosure

Environmental reports and audits are introduced. Additional sources of internal and external information are then specified, many of which students should be able to use in their research.

Pathways for enquiry

An analysis of company reports

The annual report and accounts of two companies can be analysed and compared for the nature and level of their disclosure. The companies selected could be rivals in the same industry (e.g. Sainsbury's/Tesco/Argyll) or representatives from different sectors. All major aspects of disclosure could be considered – quantitative and qualitative.

Calculation of key ratios

All the key ratios for two or more chosen firms can be calculated using their published accounts. Again, the firms could be from a single industry or from a range of industries. If the option of a wider inter-firm comparison is chosen, then the number of ratios explored could be fewer. Students should then attempt to explain possible reasons for the differences and similarities between ratios.

Company in crisis

The idea here is to investigate a crisis situation with the benefit of hindsight. Where the firm is still extant, there should be no real problem in obtaining the data but Polly Peck or Coloroll are no longer able to help! The nearest business library with back numbers of accounts may be the best answer. Students should try to find the earliest possible evidence of the firm's impending crisis and trace this forward to the period of greatest difficulty. The source of the trouble and its causes should be analysed as fully as possible.

An alternative summary

The student should use one real annual report/accounts to produce their own 'alternative' summary – one that they consider to be nearer the truth. This would be worth wordprocessing carefully and could deliberately adopt the format and style of the original. It is an opportunity to strip away all the glossy optimism of a company report and explain what has *really* happened over the year. The chairman's statement could be decoded and there can be a frank commentary on the financial statements, which can themselves be summarised with salient points highlighted. Remember that there is a great deal of potentially interesting detail hidden in notes to the accounts.

Analysis of company data

All that is needed for this investigation is the report of a company that includes a ten-year financial summary. If any back numbers of reports for the same company are available, then the time series may be traced even further back. A detailed analysis should be produced of the data available, revealing key trends and being careful to make appropriate allowance for inflation, changes in accounting practice or major changes in the firm's structure, e.g. mergers, divestments, etc. IT may be helpful in processing and presenting the material. Use could also be made of the Nuffield Data and Investigations disk. Some attempt should be made to explain reasons for significant trends and turning points in the data series.

AGM roleplay

Try holding a mock annual general meeting for a plc. The company can be real or fictitious. If a real firm is chosen, then the current (or an earlier) annual report and accounts can be used for the agenda and documentation. A fictitious scenario and accounts could be drawn from a case study or might even be devised by the students. In any case, directors with specific titles/portfolios should be appointed, including a chief executive and chair. The remainder of the students can be shareholders, probably including two or three institutional fund managers. A clear agenda should be distributed in advance. Directors should prepare short speeches and try to anticipate questions. Shareholders will study the report and accounts as the basis for some searching questions. Proceedings must be fairly formal.

Useful sources

➤ *Understanding Company Accounts* by Bob Rothenberg and John Newman (Kogan Page, 4th edn, 1994) is one of the best in this field.
➤ *Understanding Company Financial Statements* by

R. H. Parker (Penguin, 4th edn, 1994) is also excellent.

➤ *Understanding Company Accounts* by Peter Bird and Brian Rutherford (Pitman, 3rd edn, 1989) is another possible choice but a new edition is needed.

➤ *Interpreting Company Reports and Accounts* by Geoffrey Holmes and Alan Sugden (Woodhead Faulkner, 4th edn, 1990 plus recent revisions) is more detailed, but very clear and superb for teacher reference.

For analysis of accounts there are also many good titles, including most of those already mentioned.

➤ *Accounting for Non-Accountants* by Graham Mott (Pan, 1988) is very accessible.

➤ Chapter 9 in *Accounting and Financial Decisions* by David Myddelton (Longman, 1991) is still one of the best treatments.

➤ For more depth and detail *Accounting for Non-Accounting Students* by J. R. Dyson (Pitman, 1987) is useful.

➤ Superb on window dressing and corporate deception is *Accounting for Growth* by Terry Smith (Century Business, 1992).

It is strongly recommended that a library of company reports is built up, with the students making the necessary requests. Barring nationalised industries (an irony indeed!), they are all free and some firms will send out bulk orders and even back numbers. Student-favoured companies with particularly helpful and interesting reports include Cadbury-Schweppes, United Biscuits, ICI, Unilever and BP. The City Business Library (1 Brewers Hall Gardens, London EC2V 5BX) has copies of the annual reports (inspection only) for all public companies and similar libraries will be found in most cities. University business schools are another potential resource. The Financial Reporting Council (Holborn Hall, 100 Gray's Inn Road, London WC1X 8AL, Tel: 0171-404 8818) has some useful material.

Most of the major accountancy partnerships are very well disposed towards educational enquiries

and a local branch may well agree to meet students and/or offer a school/college presentation. Many small local partnerships are also likely to be suitable. The Institute of Chartered Accountants (Chartered Accountants' Hall, Moorgate Place, Moorgate EC2 2BJ, Tel: 0171-920 8100) is very helpful. Some outstanding work on ratio analysis is available from Lloyds Bowmaker (Finance House, 51 Holdenhurst Road, Bournemouth BH8 8EP). Press comment in the City pages should be monitored by all students and CD-ROM usually produces a manageable response when a major company name is entered.

Enquiry 3: How is a firm accountable internally ?

This enquiry is partly technical and partly an open debate. There is no expectation that students will make a substantial study of management accounting techniques. Certainly, the ability to carry out a simple ratio analysis and an understanding of the variance principle are important but familiarity with, say, standard costing approaches is not needed. A more qualitative appreciation of the role of the management accountant is generally envisaged. Otherwise, there is much up for debate and original enquiry. There is some fascinating case study material from the late 1980s and 1990s – such as Virgin, Next, Amstrad, Brent Walker and Maxwell Communications. The whole theme is likely to remain topical and is increasingly the subject of research and publications.

Synopsis

The opening evidence is intended to highlight the gap between the classic theory of the firm and the nature of contemporary reality. The issue of popular capitalism is raised and there is then a brief consideration of recent changes in the character of employee representation.

1 Directors and managers

The first section looks at the basic responsibilities

of business management. The role of directors is then isolated with critical commentary on their appointment, background, culture and rewards. This topic opens the problem of director accountability and shows how the influence of shareholders becomes increasingly indistinct with growth in the scale and complexity of the modern corporation.

2 Management accounts

The concept of management accounting is distinguished from the financial reporting practices already encountered. The need for management accounts is illustrated and examples are provided of the kind of questions that management accounts might answer. The basic principles of budgeting are then explained with an extended case example which refers back to the students' knowledge of breakeven analysis and contribution costing. There is simple coverage of variances. The section ends with the problems of 'information overload' and the dangers of an excessively mechanistic and quantitative culture among managers.

3 Shareholders

The section explains the formal status and rights of shareholders but also shows that most private shareholders have little or no ability, or inclination, to influence decisions within the companies that they 'own'. The issues of shareholder action groups and ethical investment are highlighted.

4 Employees

The basic relationship between employee and employer is explored and the emergence of the trade unions is briefly recounted. Pluralist and unitary views of industrial relations are explained and there is then specific coverage of recent changes in the character of the trade union movement. This leads into an explanation of the human resources (HR) approach to people management and the trend towards increased delegation through 'flatter' hierarchies. The concept of participation is outlined and reference is

made to the social chapter and to employee share ownership. The section ends with a discussion of low pay and the issue of equal opportunities.

Pathways for enquiry

The extent of directors' power

This enquiry would try to assess whether there is any limit to the power of directors. For public companies it will be necessary to consult published sources. Naturally, in a local private company the identity of directors and shareholders is likely to be much closer. What constraints still act on directors? Ideally, some broader questions could be addressed. Do managers take instructions or exercise power in their own right? What other organisations may limit director power?

Availability of information

The aim would be to find out how far companies make available information to their managers. The use of secondary sources would be one approach but an interview with a company accountant could be very revealing. It would also be valuable to have an honest discussion with one or more current or former managers. Did they experience any shortfall in the information that they needed? Did they ever feel 'kept in the dark'? Such issues are worth investigating.

The power of shareholders

The focus here should be on public companies. The *legal* power of shareholders is already considerable. The problem is that it is very difficult to deploy and hardly ever used. Legal changes could be proposed. More improvised methods of shareholders, combining their voting and questioning powers, could be explored. Existing pressure groups can be consulted. The agenda is open.

Managerial loyalty

Try to explore the problem: to what or whom is management loyal? Formally, managers report to their superiors on a scalar chain which leads ultimately to the board of directors. In reality, managers are often caught in a crossfire of conflicting claims for their loyalty. Secondary sources could form the basis for this enquiry but some primary research might be possible with managers in a range of local organisations, including the public and voluntary sectors.

Employee representation

This is an enquiry into the nature and effectiveness of employee representation. Most firms claim that the views and ideas of their employees are heard and taken into account. Students could either explore a national firm or a local enterprise. In the case of a national firm, enquiries could be made about formal policies for employee representation, union recognition, etc. In some cases, these might even be tested by talking to junior staff at the firm concerned. Caution must clearly be used in interpreting outcomes and results. A local enquiry would need the full co-operation of management but, again, could try to compare formal structures and policies with the judgement and experience of employees.

A firm's accountability to its employees

The student group might run a role-play exercise to explore the accountability of a firm to its employees. This could be based around any major strategic decision taken by the management – cutbacks and redundancies, automation and deskilling, relocation, etc. A simulated meeting could then be arranged between representatives of the workforce and the management, where statements can be made, questions asked and, perhaps, agreements reached. The role play could be run more than once, giving students the chance to take up more than one position.

An investigation of employee potential

This should be an investigation to find out why either women or an ethnic minority may fail to fulfil their true potential within business organisations. Use can be made of press reports and published sources while it could be useful to contact some pressure groups, trade unions and the Equal Opportunities Commission. It is important that the overall approach be analytical and unbiased.

Useful sources

➤ J. K. Galbraith is a well-known commentator on corporate behaviour. His *The Culture of*

Contentment (Penguin, 1992) is very readable but more depth is included in the older book *The New Industrial State* (Penguin, 1969).

➤ *An Introduction to Business Ethics* by G. D. Chryssides and J. H. Kaler (Chapman & Hall, 1993) is thoughtful and includes case studies.

➤ *Introducing Management* by Peter Lawrence and Ken Elliott (Penguin, 1985) has some useful chapters.

➤ *Writers on Organisations* by D. S. Pugh and D. J. Hickson (Penguin, 4th edn, 1989) has useful summaries on the views of famous management theorists.

➤ There are innumerable books on management accounting but *Management Accounting* by Graham Mott (Pan, 1987) is very clear.

➤ The excellent *Understanding Company Accounts* by Bob Rothenberg and John Newman (Kogan Page, 4th edn, 1994) is a gentle introduction.

➤ For shareholder power, a radical but absolutely invaluable book is *The Shareholder's Action Guide* by Craig Mackenzie (New Consumer, 1993).

➤ Particularly recommended for employee affairs are *British Industrial Relations* by Howard F. Gospel and Gill Palmer (Routledge, 2nd edn, 1993) and *A Handbook of Human Resource Management* by Michael Armstrong (Kogan Page, 1988).

➤ CD-ROM enquiries on the Cadbury Report are worthwhile.

Useful organisations include:
➤ Institute of Directors (116 Pall Mall, London SW1Y 5EA, Tel: 0171-839 1233)
➤ Institute of Chartered Accountants (Chartered Accountants' Hall, Moorgate Place, Moorgate, London EC2 2BJ, Tel: 0171-920 8100)
➤ Institute of Internal Auditors (33 Abbeville Mews, 88 Clapham Park Road, London SW4 7BX, Tel: 0171-498 0101)
➤ Institutional Investors (56 Kingsway, London WC2B 6DX, Tel: 0171-430 0881)
➤ New Consumer (52 Elswick Road, Newcastle-upon-Tyne NE4 6JH, Tel: 0191-272 1148)
➤ The UK Shareholders' Association (Half Tiles, Roseacre Gardens, Chilworth, Nr Guildford GU4 8RQ)

➤ Ethical Investment Research Service (504 Bondway Business Centre, 71 Bondway, London SW8 1SQ, Tel: 0171-735 1351)

➤ Trades Union Congress (Great Russell Street, London WC1B 3LS, Tel: 0171-636 4030)

Enquiry 4: How is a firm accountable to its creditors, suppliers and customers?

This enquiry examines the nature of accountability through contractual relationships outside the firm. The subject of loan creditors moves from the evidence of the balance sheet to the issues of bank finance for business, overtrading and gearing. Accountability in the supplier–customer relationship is looked at from both sides and is linked to the concepts of lean production and total quality. Finally, the legal framework of accountability towards consumers is set alongside the pressure of market forces to ensure consumer satisfaction. It is important that the subject areas of this enquiry are not treated merely as discrete entities but are related to the underlying themes of stakeholders and competitive advantage.

Synopsis

The opening evidence raises some of the key contemporary issues in the fast-changing picture of contractual accountability. New evidence can readily be introduced or students can find additional material for themselves.

1 Loan creditors

The nature of short- and long-term liabilities is highlighted through extracts from the balance sheet for a large and a small company. This leads to consideration of loan finance from banks and the relationship between the bank and the borrower. Expansion and the risk of overtrading introduces the question of gearing and debt: equity structures.

2 Suppliers

The section begins with the traditional issues of credit control and liquidity while raising the problem of supplier dependency. The focus then shifts to the contemporary theme of how supplier relationships are being radically changed by the needs of lean production systems and total quality management.

3 Customers

Statutory and voluntary approaches to consumer protection are briefly explained. The extent to which customers are protected by the competitive energy of market forces is discussed and the idea of customer satisfaction is related to ultimate business success.

Pathways for enquiry

An enquiry into the adequacy of bank loans to business

The marketing literature of all the high street banks stresses the availability of business loans. Yet many entrepreneurs maintain that the banks fail to support sound business plans, preferring to use their funds to offer consumer credit. A possible starting point for the investigation would be the banks' marketing literature. Some local business opinion could then be compared with the view of one or more branch banks. The national picture could be explored using CD-ROM and secondary sources.

Bank–business customer relationships

How far do bank managers affect business managers? Indebtedness creates obligation. This enquiry should investigate the extent to which the reality of indebtedness to banks affects business decision making – in its atmosphere and actuality. It will be most revealing if the experience of both sides is researched and contrasted. In most cases, a focus on a small business will be more effective and more practical.

Supplier–customer relationships

This should be an investigation into recent and current change in the supplier–customer relationship. It should be possible to find out how the relative emphasis on price and quality have changed. Are there any other dimensions in the link that have become important, e.g. stability? How critical is competitive quoting? Have personal relationships with suppliers become more significant? Ideally, this investigation will be directed towards a local business but there are also many articles and books on the wider national and international scenario.

Consumer protection

This enquiry should try to evaluate any specific form of consumer protection, e.g. the regulation of advertising or the provision of consumer credit. The extent of present protection can be compared with views of consumers (a small survey?), the Trading Standards Department and a pressure group such as the Consumers' Association. These opinions might be contrasted with those of a relevant producer, a manufacturers' association, a chamber of commerce or even the CBI.

The level of customer satisfaction

This enquiry is about why and how a firm may increase the level of customer satisfaction. One firm and one product will probably be most suitable. The example chosen should be simple and *small in scale*. National or local firms and goods or services are all equally valid. The initial sources of customer satisfaction should be uncovered. The reasons for an effort to increase customer satisfaction can be analysed. Then the strategy to achieve that increase should be examined and evaluated. Finally, some critical assessment could be attempted. What was the cost of increased consumer satisfaction? How far were the firm's objectives realised? Did this affect the firm's efficiency in the use of resources?

Useful sources

➤ *Lloyds Bank Small Business Guide* (Penguin, 1994) is useful on loan creditors.
➤ *The Independent* (26 May 1994) published an excellent 'special' on credit management.
➤ *Building Customer Loyalty* by Ian Linton (Pitman, 1993) is accessible and very good on supplier relationships.

➤ The Consumers Association is clearly invaluable as a source on consumer protection (2 Marylebone Road, London NW1 4DF, Tel: 0171-830 6000)

Useful organisations include:
➤ The Consumer Choice (162 Regent Street, London W1R 5TB, Tel: 0171-734 7005).
➤ The Department of Trade and Industry (1–19 Victoria Street, London SW1, Tel: 0171-215 5000)
➤ Office of Fair Trading (Field House, Breams Buildings, London EC4A 1PR, Tel: 0171-242 2858)
➤ The Advertising Standards Authority (Brook House, Torrington Place, London WC1, Tel: 0171-580 5555)
➤ The local council Trading Standards Department.

Enquiry 5: Is business accountable to the world around?

This final enquiry is directed outwards into the society and world where business organisations operate. The opening area of concern is the local communities within which firms are physically based. This focus then widens to address the problems of transnational enterprise. The theme of environmental responsibility follows, with consideration of how market forces may act in both adverse and benign ways. In the last section there is a broad discussion regarding the ways in which business enterprise affects the overall quality of life.

Synopsis

The opening evidence illustrates some of the recently enhanced expectations of business. These contrast with such difficult questions as extreme inequality, environmental damage and an arguably materialistic and consumerist culture.

1 The community

The realities of relationships between firms and the

communities in which they operate are briefly recounted. The variable response of companies to the claims of the community is charted and this leads to discussing the social effects of closures and withdrawals of business activity. The concept of business accountability to the national interest is briefly considered.

2 Transnational enterprise

The section starts by illustrating the scale and significance of transnationals. This introduces the motives of firms in developing a transnational identity. The problem of double standards is discussed and the imbalances of power relations are illustrated. Some signposts are offered to the complex ethical questions that arise from this topic.

3 The environment

The section starts with a brief historical background to the environmental debate with illustration of the major issues. Assessment follows of the role of the price mechanism in determining environmental impacts and the problems of its application to externalities. Environmental taxes and the concept of tradable permits are considered. Finally, there is illustration of the sharply differing responses made by firms to increased national and international concern.

4 The quality of life?

This section examines the broad impact of business activity on culture and society at large. The nature of market relationships is explored and questions are raised about the materialistic tendencies of a modern industrial society. How far is the market an unstoppable ratchet in its demands on the natural environment? Does the market have any power to distinguish adequately products that are ethically acceptable or socially desirable? Has the quality of life risen or fallen in response to economic growth and the cumulative achievements of business? Has business delivered what people want or do people merely want what business delivers?

Pathways for enquiry

An evaluation of the accountability of business to the local community

It might be possible to contrast the stated attitudes of firms with some evidence of their commitment to date. Rotary Clubs, traders' associations and the local press may all be useful points of reference on this subject.

How far is business accountable to the national interest?

It would be useful to look at past performance. Have the largest enterprises accepted any particular national obligations? Are firms expected by government to show any national loyalty when making business decisions? Do business leaders believe that they have any debt to Britain? Do ordinary people expect such loyalty and on what grounds? For the most part, this enquiry would need to use secondary sources, particularly press coverage of high-profile decisions, e.g. the British Aerospace sale of Rover to BMW.

The extent of a transnational's accountability

This enquiry should assess the extent to which a transnational is accountable outside its country of origin. A focus would be the policies and behaviour of a large transnational with significant operations in the UK. This might have the UK as its exclusive or joint country of origin (e.g. BP or Unilever) or might have entered the UK to set up a subsidiary enterprise (e.g. Ford or Toshiba). The enquiry might consider accountability to the local population, to employees, to the 'host' government or to the natural environment.

The effect of market forces on environmental accountability

This could be explored at any level or for any type of business enterprise. The enquiry should try to test and balance two basic arguments. First is the idea that the twin needs, to minimise costs and increase sales, drive firms to exploit the environment with inadequate concern for the future. The alternative argument suggests that firms are motivated by markets to protect the environment through pressure from individual consumer choice and from public opinion in general.

Is what is good for business also good for society?

This is a very open investigation, likely to encounter some strongly held and opposing views. It would be interesting to consult some representatives of business, trade unions, political parties, the local council and pressure groups. Public opinion might also be tested. An alternative, more practical approach might assess the overall impact of a local business initiative. This might be quite small in scope – for example, the opening of a take-away food outlet.

Useful sources

The main problem for these areas is the sheer weight and diversity of material. There is also a risk that the debate can become one-sided as case material tends to be more readily available from pressure groups critical of business than from firms themselves or from pro-business organisations.

➤ *Corporate Responsibility* by Tom Cannon, (Pitman, 1992); Sections 3 and 4 are very helpful for the teacher.

➤ *Good Business? Case Studies in Corporate Social Responsibility* (Centre for Social Management/School for Advanced Urban Studies/New Consumer, 1993) is invaluable.

➤ *Business and Society* by Edmund Marshall (Routledge, 1993) is heavier but worth having in the library.

➤ *Applied Economics* by A. Griffiths and S. Wall (Longman, 5th edn, 1993) is surprisingly useful.

➤ *Multinationals* by Richard Crum and Stephen Davies (Heinemann, 1991) is very suitable for students.

➤ *Sociology of the Global System* by Leslie Sklair (Harvester Wheatsheaf, 1991) is serious but approachable.

➤ *How the Other Half Dies* by Susan George (Penguin, 1976) is a classic.

➤ *The Global Consumer* by Phil Wells and Mandy Jetter (Gollancz, 1991) has plenty of practical information.

There are some interesting books on 'green' issues including:

➤ *Green Business* by Malcolm Wheatley (Pitman, 1993).

➤ *Friends of the Earth Handbook* ed. by Jonathan Porritt (Optima, 1987) – very useful for references.

➤ *The Green Business Guide* by John Elkington et al. (Gollancz, 1992).

➤ *Future Wealth* by James Robertson (Cassell, 1990).

➤ *The Myth of the Market* by Jeremy Seabrook (Green Books, 1990).

➤ More philosophical but classic is Eric Fromm's *To Have or To Be?* (Abacus, 1978).

➤ *Small is Beautiful* by Fritz Schumacher (Abacus, 1972) is always worthwhile.

Useful organisations include:

➤ Business in the Community (8 Stratton Street, London W1X 5FD, Tel: 0171-629 1600)

➤ Oxfam (274 Banbury Road, Oxford OX2 7DZ, Tel: (01865) 311311)

➤ Traidcraft (Kingsway, Gateshead, Tyne and Wear NE11 0NE)

➤ World Development Movement (25 Beehive Place, Brixton, London SW9 7QR, Tel: 0171-737 6215)

➤ Friends of the Earth (26–28 Underwood Street, London N1 7JQ, Tel: 0171-490 1555)

➤ Greenpeace (Canonbury Villas, London N1 2PN, Tel: 0171-354 5100)

➤ Ark Environmental Foundation (8–10 Bourdon Street, London W1X 9HX, Tel: 0171-409 2638)

➤ Schumacher Society – ask for their excellent catalogue of useful books (Ford House, Hartland, Bideford, Devon EX39 6EE, Tel: (01237) 441621)

Appendix: Using Microsoft® Excel for Windows™

Microsoft Excel version 4.0 is a powerful and versatile automated business tool which can be used for calculations, data analysis, projections, decision making and reporting.

It can be used as a spreadsheet or database and can produce charts and diagrams. It can hold and process vast amounts of information and perform intricate calculations. It is compatible with Lotus 1-2-3 spreadsheet program and data from one program can be transferred to the other.

Spreadsheets and charts can be placed directly into word-processed documents.

Spreadsheets

A spreadsheet is a grid made up of rows and columns. Each square in the grid is called a **CELL** (or slot) and each cell's position on the grid is identified by its cell reference, i.e. the row and column in which it appears.

Data are entered on to the spreadsheet in a planned and ordered layout to build up a matrix of information. Both text and numerical data can be entered.

Spreadsheets are normally used as a tool for dealing with figures and calculations, e.g. accounting, stock-keeping, etc, with text headings and labels.

Formulae can be built into the spreadsheet so that the whole table can be recalculated automatically if any of the data in it are changed.

Excel runs through an application called Windows which allows you to switch from Excel to other applications and back again without quitting the Excel program.

Excel needs a minimum of a 286 processor running MS-DOS version 3.1 or later, Windows version 3.0 or later in standard or enhanced mode and at least 2 MB of random access memory (RAM).

To load Excel

From Program Manager, double click on the Excel icon in the Applications group.

A blank Excel worksheet will appear on screen.

Using the mouse

Excel can be operated using the keyboard *or* the mouse. In this lesson instructions are given for the mouse which is the quickest and easiest method.

Unless specified otherwise, actions are carried out using the mouse by clicking once on the left-hand button.

To move the pointer around the screen, simply move the mouse around the desktop until the pointer on screen is in the correct position.

Note: In this lesson >> means 'do this'. Every time you see this symbol, carry out the directions that follow.

Whenever you see the command ENTER in the lesson, this means press the ENTER key.

>> Load Excel.

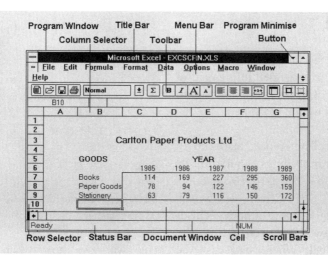

Example of an Excel worksheet

The screen you see when you load Excel is the basic worksheet and will look similar to the one shown above.

The areas of the screen that you need to be familiar with are:

1 The Menu Bar

This is the area where you choose which command or operation you would like to carry out.

For the moment, File, Edit, Formula and Format are the ones you will need to use most.

>> Move the pointer to the word File in the Menu Bar and click on the mouse.

A pull-down menu will appear and you are presented with the various commands that are available to you in the File menu.

>> Click on the word File again to clear the menu and try looking at the other menus.

2 The Toolbar

The Toolbar – see below – contains buttons which give shortcut ways to carry out some of the commands you will use in Excel.

3 The Formula Bar

Below the Menu Bar is the Formula Bar. When you start to use the worksheet you will see that what you type on to the sheet will appear in the formula bar as well as on the worksheet.

You can use this to check the accuracy of your input, especially if you are building up formulae.

The Toolbar

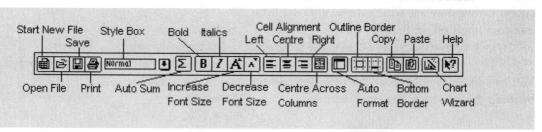

4 The worksheet

This is the main area of the spreadsheet where you will enter all your data. It is divided into a grid of cells. Data (text or numbers) are entered into each cell individually to build up the worksheet.

Each cell has its own cell reference, made up of row headings and column headings to pinpoint its place on the worksheet, e.g. A1, B16, F93, etc.

One cell (A1) has a bold outline around it. This is the CURSOR. It shows that cell A1 is the **ACTIVE CELL** or cell where data will be entered or edited when you start to type at the keyboard.
>> Type something into the cell and press ENTER.

If you make a mistake when entering data, the backspace key will cancel what you have just typed and then you can type the correction.

Moving around the worksheet

To move the cursor around the worksheet, just move the mouse pointer around the screen and click on the cell you wish to select.
>> Try moving the cursor around the worksheet and selecting individual cells.

As you do this notice that the active cell reference shown at the left end of the formula bar changes and always shows the active cell reference.

You can move beyond the limits of the document on screen by clicking the mouse on the up, down, left or right pointing arrows in the scroll bars (see diagram). If you hold your finger on the mouse button the window will scroll continuously until you take your finger off the button.
>> Try moving the cursor to cell Y42 using the scroll bars.

You can move rapidly around a large spreadsheet by using the following key combinations.

HOME key	to move to the beginning of a row.
END key	to move to the end of a row.
PAGE UP key	to move up one screen (or window).
PAGE DOWN key	to move down one screen.
CONTROL + HOME keys together	to move to the top left of the document.
CONTROL + END keys together	to move to the bottom right of the document.
CONTROL + DIRECTION keys together	to move to the edge of the data block.

This will save time when working on a large document, particularly if you bear in mind that Excel has the capacity for 256 columns and 16384 rows.

>> Try using the key combinations to move around the document.

In a very large spreadsheet, the **GOTO** command is very useful.

>> Select Formula from the Menu Bar.
   Select Goto.
   Type the cell reference in the dialogue box that appears, e.g. C197
   ENTER.

The cursor will move to cell C197.

Working on a spreadsheet

Entering data

Select the cell where you wish to enter the data, simply type it in and ENTER.

Clearing a cell

Highlight the cell.
Press the delete key.
A dialogue box will open, requesting which cell attribute you wish to clear.
Select All.
Select OK.

If you only want to clear one particular attribute of the cell, e.g. formulae, select formula in the dialogue box and select OK. In this case the contents will remain but the formulae which applied to the cell will be cleared.

>> Clear cell A1

To edit the contents of a cell

If you want to amend some data in a cell but do not need to clear the whole cell:

Select the cell to be edited.

Activate the Formula bar by moving the cursor into the formula bar and clicking on the mouse at the point where you want to make amendments.

Type the amendments.

ENTER.

To undo an error

If you make a mistake and issue a wrong command, you may be able to reverse the error by using the Undo command.

Select Edit.

Select Undo.

This will undo only the last command unless it is a command that cannot be undone, in which case a screen message will tell you so.

Creating a worksheet

Follow the instructions below to build up a spreadsheet, enter data, build formulae, edit data, format the spreadsheet, save the spreadsheet on disk and print the spreadsheet.

When you have finished you should know enough about Excel to go on to other exercises where you can build up spreadsheets on your own.

Before you start you should have a rough outline of what information you need to include and how you want your spreadsheet to look. This will save time spent making changes later.

Look at the table below:

Quarterly Total

>> Move to cell A1 and type SW Regional Sales 1989 and ENTER.

You will see that the text is too long for one cell and spills over into the next. As you do not need to use cells B1 and C1 this does not matter.

>> Move the cursor down to cell A3, type Salesperson and ENTER.

>> Move the cursor down to cell A5.

Excel spreadsheets are usually built up by creating **RANGES** and entering data into these ranges. A range is a block of joined cells which contain related data.

SW Regional Sales 1993						
Salesperson	**March**	**June**	**Sept**	**Dec**	**Individual Total**	**Annual Commission 5%**
Alice BLAKE	10565	26755	13600	19600		
Martin CLAYTON	19400	17660	66405	16700		
Mark HASCOMBE	14345	18300	20500	22455		
Sally JENKINS	30700	45775	20355	14300		
Michael REECE	45855	30625	14555	17600		
Howard SIMPSON	11945	16700	18500	20950		

Creating a range

To create a range, move the cursor to the first cell in the range, hold your finger down on the button and drag the mouse across the cells you want to include in the range. Release the button when all relevant cells have been selected.

>> With the cursor in cell A5 press and hold down the button. Drag the mouse pointer down to A10 and release the button.

The first cell in the range remains highlighted. This is the active cell.

Within a range, once data has been entered into a cell, the cursor automatically moves to the next cell in the range.

>> With A5 as the active cell, type Alice Blake and press enter.
>> Enter the other salespersons' names into cells A6 to A10.

To remove or cancel the range highlighted press one of the direction arrow keys or select another cell.

The default cell size is 12.75 points high by 8.43 units wide, which is too small. Some of the names have spilled over into the adjoining cell. As you need to use the cells in column B you must make column A wider to accommodate the full names.

To do this, place your cursor in the column heading row right on the column boundary that you want to move. The cursor will become a cross with arrows pointing left and right. Press and hold down the mouse button and drag the column boundary until the column is wide enough to accommodate the widest cell of data. Release the button.

>> Make column A the appropriate width.
>> Select cell B3 and create a range from B3 to E3.
    Enter the headings March, June, Sept and Dec along the top of the columns.
    Select cell F2. Type Individual. ENTER.
    Select cell F3. Type Total. ENTER.

>> Enter the other row and column headings from the table.
>> Select cell B5. Create a range to include cells B5 to E10.
    Enter figures into these cells from the table.

Building formulae

There are several ways to build a formula. The easiest is to use functions.

>> Place the cursor in the cell where you want the answer to the calculation to go, i.e. B12.
    Type =
    Type SUM(B5:B10) (*The colon indicates a range.*)
    ENTER.

SUM is the function.

Note: A formula *must always* start with = This is how Excel recognises that what you are typing is a formula.

Some other common functions are:

AVERAGE	to find the average.
SQRT	to find the square root.
MAX	to find the largest number.
MIN	to find the smallest number.
STDEV	to find the standard deviation.

Using functions can save time when performing extensive calculations.

Complex formulae can be built up using a combination of functions and operators, e.g. =SUM(A2:A40)*117.5% will work out the total of a column of figures (A2 to A40) and add 17.5% VAT to the total.

The more common formula operators are:

% (per cent sign)	percent
* (asterisk)	multiplication
/ (slash)	division
+ (plus sign)	addition
− (minus sign)	subtraction

There is a SUM button on the Toolbar. If the formula is a straightforward sum, select the cell where the total should go and click on the SUM button. A range will be suggested. If this is correct, click on the SUM button again. If the suggested range is incorrect, drag the cursor over the correct range and click the SUM button again.

On your spreadsheet you now need to use the same formula that you built above for the June, Sept. and Dec. totals.

Instead of building up a new formula for each total, you can copy the formula for the March total across to the other columns.

To copy a formula

>> Select cell B12 which contains the formula you wish to copy.
Select Edit from the Menu Bar.
Select Copy.
Now select cell C12 (you will notice a dotted border or marquee remains around cell B12).
Create a range from C12 to E12.
Select Edit.
Select Paste.

The formula has been copied across and all the totals have been automatically entered.

These formulae will now always refer to these cells and every time a figure on the table is changed the totals will automatically be recalculated.
>> Now select cell F5 and build up a formula for the total individual sales for Alice Blake.
>> Copy this formula down from cell F5 to cell F12.

Next you need to work out the annual commission for each salesperson.
>> Select cell G5 and build up a formula for working out commission at 5%.
Type =
Type F5*5%
ENTER.

The commission total should appear.
>> Copy this formula down for the rest of the sales staff.
>> Now try changing Alice Blake's sales for Sept and see how all the other totals are recalculated.

Formatting the spreadsheet

You have finished entering data on the spreadsheet.

You can now alter the appearance of the spreadsheet to suit your needs, i.e. text size and type, alignment of data within cells, row height, borders, etc.

The commands for changing the look of the worksheet are contained in the Format Menu. Alternatively, the spreadsheet can be formatted using the Toolbar.
>> Select cell F3.
Select Format.
Select Alignment.

A dialogue box appears on screen with the options for cell alignment available to you.
>> Select Centre in the Horizontal Alignment box.
Select OK.

The heading has now been centred in the cell. This could also be achieved by selecting the cell and clicking on the Centre Align button in the Toolbar.
>> Centre the headings in cell G2 and cell G3.

To alter the font size and style

>> Select cell A1.
Select Format.
Select Font.
Select Helv in the Font box.
Select 14 in the Size box.
Select Bold in the Font Style box.
Select Underline in the Effects box.
Select OK.

There are buttons in the Toolbar for emboldening, italicising, increasing and decreasing font size and aligning text to the left, right and centre of the cell. Select the cells you want to format before clicking on the buttons.

Borders and backgrounds

You can add borders or shading to cells or ranges of cells.

>> Select cells B5 to E10.
>> Select Format.
Select Border.
Select Outline in the Border box.
Select the solid single line in the style box.
Select OK.

>> Select cells B5 to E10 again.
Select Format.
Select Patterns.
Click on the arrow following the Pattern box.
Click on a light stippled pattern.
Click on OK.

There are buttons in the Toolbar for placing borders or outlines around cells or blocks of cells. First select the cells that you want to apply borders to.

Formatting numbers

In this worksheet all the figures used have been whole numbers and have appeared on screen just as you have typed them.

The format in which the numbers appear can be changed by using the Format Numbers command.

>> Select cells B5 to G12.
Select Format.
Select Number.

A dialogue box opens with a selection of number formats displayed.

>> Select Currency in the Category box.
Select £#,##0, the first option in the Format Codes box.
Select OK.

All numbers should now be displayed in this format.

Formatting layout

You may wish to insert blank rows or columns into your spreadsheet to improve its presentation or to add further rows or columns of data.

To insert a row/column

Click on the row or column heading where you want the new row/column to go.
Select Edit.
Select Insert.

To delete a row/column

Select the row/column you want to delete by clicking on the row/column heading.
Select Edit.
Select Delete.

>> Insert a blank column at column F.
>> Place the cursor in the row heading bar and move it to the junction of rows A13 and A14 until the cursor becomes a cross with arrows pointing left and right. Press and hold down the mouse button and drag the row border until row A13 is double the height of the other rows.
Release the button.

This will leave a distinct break between the S.W. Sales table and the next table which you can now enter starting at cell A14.

>> Using the S.W. Sales spreadsheet as a guide, make up a similar one for N.E. Sales using the information below. Use ranges, formulae and copying when constructing your spreadsheet and then try formatting the spreadsheet to your own design.

Michael ELLIOTT	16400	12895	23610	19505
Terry SMITH	24280	12710	18450	15800
Edward KELLY	17650	31000	20650	24850
Sheila MACLEOD	19190	28110	22750	26200
Lawrence SELBY	18490	17680	21250	27770
Catherine SMART	37400	16450	25950	23850

>> Build a formula to give a Grand Total of N.E. and S.W. Sales in an appropriate cell.

To save a spreadsheet on to a disk

Select File.

Select Save As.

When the dialogue box opens click on the arrow following the drives box.

Click on A in the list that appears to save the spreadsheet on the disk in drive A.

Type a name for your file in the File Name box (e.g. Sales).

ENTER.

\>> Save your Sales file on to disk.

To clear a file from the screen

Select File.

Select Close.

You may be asked if you want to save any changes made, if so answer yes or no as appropriate.

To start a new worksheet

Select File.

Select New.

Select Worksheet.

Select OK.

or

Click on the New Worksheet button in the Toolbar.

To exit from Excel

Select File.

Select Exit.

To load a file from disk

Load Excel.

When the Excel worksheet has loaded select File.

Select Open (*or* click on the Open File button in the Toolbar).

Click on the arrow following the Drives box.

Click on A.

Click on the file you want to load in the File Name list box.

ENTER.

Printing a spreadsheet

Select File.

Select Print (*or* click on the Print button in the Toolbar).

Before printing you can view on screen how the printed document will look.

Click in the Preview box.

Click on OK.

Select Zoom to see a magnified view of the page (cancel by selecting zoom again).

Select Close to return to the original document.

or

Select Print to print the spreadsheet.

If your spreadsheet is too wide to fit on to A4 paper used lengthways (portrait) you can print widthways (landscape). To do this:

Select File.

Select Print.

Select Page Setup.

Select Printer Setup.

Select Setup.

Select Landscape in the Orientation box.

ENTER.

ENTER.

Select Print.

\>> Print the spreadsheet that you have just created.

Printing part of a spreadsheet

You can print only a selected part of a spreadsheet if you wish.

Select or highlight the part of the spreadsheet that you want to print.

Select Options.

Select Set Print Area.

Select File.

Select Print.

ENTER.

The Set Print Area command must be removed before the whole spreadsheet or a different part of it can be printed.

Select the whole spreadsheet by clicking on the grey button at the top left of the worksheet where the row and column headings meet.

Select Options.

Select Remove Print Area.

Relative and absolute cell references

In the Sales spreadsheet earlier, formulae were copied across using **RELATIVE CELL REFERENCES**.

For example, the formula for the total sales for Alice Blake, i.e. B5+C5+D5+E5, was automatically altered to read B6+C6+D6+E6 when copied down to calculate Martin Clayton's sales.

These cell references are called **RELATIVE CELL REFERENCES** and relate to their place on the spreadsheet. Any formula containing relative cell references will change the cell references automatically when the formula is copied elsewhere to refer to a new set of cells.

All cell references are relative unless specified otherwise.

However, in some instances you may not want a particular reference to change from one formula to the next, i.e. you wish it to remain a constant. This can be achieved by using what is called an **ABSOLUTE CELL REFERENCE**.

To designate a cell reference as absolute it must be entered into a formula by preceding both the column and the row reference by a $ (dollar) sign, e.g. A1.

>> Create a simple spreadsheet as laid out below:

	A	B	C
1	.05		Interest Rate
2			
3	£650		
4	£500		
5	£325		

Here .05 is the rate of interest (5%).

To calculate how much interest will be earned on £650, the formula B3=A3*A1 can be applied.

>> Try this now.

>> Now copy the formula down to B4 and B5.

Notice how the calculation is now incorrect because not only has A3 been altered to relate to cells A4 and A5, but A1 has also changed and does not now refer to the rate of interest in A1.

To rectify this, cell A1 must be entered as an **ABSOLUTE** (or constant) **CELL** reference in the original formula.

>> Clear cells B3 to B5.

>> In cell B3 enter the formula: =A3*A1

>> Copy this formula down to cells B4 and B5.

The interest accruing is now correct.

Remember that the $ sign must be used before both the column *and* the row reference.

Use relative cell references when you want the cell references to be updated when copying a formula. Use absolute cell references when you want a cell reference *always* to refer to the same cell.

Freezing panes

If you have a very large spreadsheet you may want to be able to see the row and column headings when you scroll down the worksheet. To do this:

Place the cursor below and to the right of the rows and columns that you want to freeze.
Select Window from the Menu Bar.
Select Freeze Pane.

Now when you scroll down the spreadsheet, the row and column headings will be held in place while the rest of the spreadsheet moves.

The following exercise contains many of the commands explained above. The answers are given on page 143.

Exercise 1

1 Start a new worksheet.

2 Create a spreadsheet using the information in the table opposite. Enter all the data, not just the table. Note that the sauna is closed on Tuesdays and Thursdays.

3 What formula must you use to find out how many people use the sauna during the week? Where should the formula go? Use suitable formulae to complete the other totals.

4 What formula must you use to find out the total number of people attending the centre on a Monday? Where should the formula go? Use suitable formulae to complete the totals for the remaining days of the week.

5 What is the formula to calculate the revenue from the sauna for the week? Complete the formulae for the Revenue row, including the Total Revenue. Use Relative and Absolute references if necessary.

6 Insert formulae to calculate the average daily usage of each facility and the average number of people using the centre each day.

7 Format the spreadsheet using bold type for the column headings and bold italics for the row headings (i.e. Monday to Sunday). Centre the headings and format monetary figures correctly.

8 Using the MAX and MIN functions, insert rows showing the maximum and minimum numbers for each facility.

9 Save the spreadsheet as ISLAND.XLS

10 Print the spreadsheet in two formats, one showing the figures and one showing the formulae.

11 Produce and fully label a bar chart showing the total weekly figures for each activity.

Island Leisure Centre

Opening hours

Monday to Friday	10.00 a.m. to 9.00 p.m.
Saturdays and Sundays	10.00 a.m. to 5.30 p.m.

Facilities	Max. no of persons
Sauna	5
(closed Tuesdays and Thursdays)	
Conditioning room	12
Squash courts	12
Swimming pool	75
Sunbeds	2

Costs (per person/per half hour)

Sauna	£2.50
Conditioning room	£2.00
Squash	£2.50
Swimming pool	£1.80
Sunbed	£2.50

Use of Island Leisure Centre for week beginning 9 September

Day	Sauna	Conditioning	Squash	Swimming Pool	Sunbed
Monday	7	105	30	600	6
Tuesday	X	150	45	800	10
Wednesday	10	150	60	700	8
Thursday	X	180	78	600	15
Friday	23	125	57	1300	12
Saturday	32	110	75	1100	24
Sunday	28	75	30	1100	20

Excel charts

Any data that have been entered on to an Excel spreadsheet can be depicted graphically on screen or printed out as a chart. You can choose from 90 types of available charts, or you can design your own by customising the available charts.

Carlton Paper Products Ltd: Growth in Sales 1985-1989					
Goods			**Year**		
	1985	**1986**	**1987**	**1988**	**1989**
Books	114	169	227	295	360
Paper goods	78	94	122	146	159
Stationery	63	79	116	150	172

For the purposes of this worksheet >> means 'do this'. Every time you see >> carry out the instructions that follow.
>> Load Excel.
>> Create a spreadsheet the same as the one shown above.

Creating a new chart

When creating a new chart you must first select the cells on the worksheet that contain the data that you want to plot. Do this using the mouse, by placing the cursor in the first cell on the spreadsheet containing data that you want to use, pressing down the mouse button and dragging the cursor across the spreadsheet until all the data you want to plot have been highlighted. Release the mouse button. Press the F11 function key. A column chart will automatically be created.
>> Select cells A6 to F9.
>> Press F11.

A column chart will appear on screen and across the top of the chart will be the Chart Menu Bar which contains all the commands relevant to the chart.

You can change the type of chart if a column format

is not the type of chart you want. Excel offers 14 different types of chart, Area, Bar, Column, Line, Pie, Scatter, Radar, Combination and 3D versions of these. Each of these has a selection of formats: a total of 90 in all.

If none of these is exactly what you want, you can choose the format that is closest to the format you need and then you can customise it to suit.

Changing chart type

The types of chart are contained in the Gallery command in the Chart Menu Bar.
>> Click on Gallery.
     Click on Pie.

A dialogue box will open showing you several types of pie chart format. By clicking on one of the formats and clicking on OK the chart will change to the pie chart format that you chose.
>> Try choosing different chart types from the Gallery Menu and selecting different formats to see which is most appropriate for your purpose, i.e. the one that best illustrates the information you are trying to depict.

Customising a chart

Once you have decided upon the chart format you wish to use, select it and customise your chart in that format.
>> Click on Gallery.
     Click on Column.
     Click on the first option.
     Click on OK.

Each chart has several characteristics. Each of these can be customised using the Chart Menus.

Excel automatically includes certain essential elements or 'chart objects' in a chart, e.g. axes, axis values, etc. These can all be formatted.

Other elements or 'chart objects' can be added or formatted to your design, e.g. legend (key), title, explanatory text, axis titles and arrows.

Customising a chart is accomplished using the **Chart** and **Format** Menus.

The chart menu

The commands in this menu allow you to add elements or objects to your chart or select the whole chart or plot area.

The format menu

The commands in this menu allow you to format the chart and chart objects and to move chart objects around the chart.

To use any Format command with a chart object, you must first select or activate it. You can do this simply by using the mouse. Point the cursor arrow at the chart object you want to select or activate and click on the left-hand mouse button. Small squares appear around the edge of the element you have selected.

If the squares are black the elements can be formatted with commands and can be moved or sized directly with the keyboard or mouse.

If the squares are white the chart objects cannot be moved or sized directly but some formatting commands can be used.

If text etc. is editable, it will appear in the formula bar at the top of the screen. You can type your revised text into the formula bar and check it before entering it on the chart.

Customise the chart on screen

The chart you see on screen is very basic and needs more explanation and clarification. Look again at the types of column chart.
>> Click on Gallery.
   Click on Column.

The fourth option shows overlapping columns which look effective when comparing two variables.
>> Click on the fourth option.
   Click on OK.

You may wish to change the column colours to a particular colour scheme.
>> Point the cursor arrow at a red column and click.
   The red columns are now selected (note the white squares that indicate this).
   Click on Format.
   Click on Patterns.
   Click on the arrow in the Border colour box.
   Click on blue.
   Click on the arrow in the Area Foreground box and click on blue. Click on the Area Pattern box and choose the 7th option (horizontal stripes).
   Click on OK.
>> Repeat for the green column, using a different blue pattern.

Click on the mouse button with the cursor arrow somewhere within the chart (*not* on the spreadsheet behind) to deselect the columns.

An explanatory heading would be useful.
>> Click on Chart.
   Click on Attach Text.
   Click on Chart Title.
   Click on OK.
   Type a title – Carlton Paper Products Ltd – it will appear in the formula bar, where you can edit it if necessary.
   Press ENTER.

Emphasise the heading. A shadow effect behind the heading makes it stand out more.
>> Select the heading.
>> Click on Format.
   Click on Patterns.
   Click on the Shadow check box.
   Click on OK.

Change font and font size for further emphasis.
>> Select the heading.

Click on Format.
Click on Font.
Click on 14 in the size box.
Click on the arrow in the font box and choose a new font style.
Click on OK.
Click to deselect the heading.

Add explanatory text for the axes.
>> Click on Chart.
   Click on Attach Text.
   Click on Value Axis.
   Click on OK.
   Type in the name for the axis (Sales).
   Press ENTER.
   Click on the button to deselect the value axis.
   Repeat for the Category Axis (Year).

If the chart is small and cramped on screen, click on the upward pointing white arrow at the extreme top right of the Chart Window to make the chart bigger.
>> Enlarge the Chart Window.

An explanatory key or legend would also be helpful.
>> Click on Chart.
   Click on Add Legend.

A legend will be pasted on to the chart. It might look more balanced if it were placed below the chart.
>> Select the legend.
   Click on Format
   Click on Legend.
   Click on Bottom.
   Click on OK.
   Click to deselect the legend.

Some gridlines on the Value Axis would indicate more easily at a glance the actual value of sales.
>> Click on Chart.
   Click on Gridlines.
   Click on the Value Axis Major Gridlines box.
   Click on OK.

Add further text to the chart.

>> Type Growth in Sales. (Note the text appearing in the formula bar.)
   Press ENTER. The text will be placed on top of your chart.
   Place the cursor on the text you have just typed, press and hold down the mouse button and drag the text to a position just below the title.
   Use the other black handles to stretch or shrink the text.

Saving a chart

Each chart is saved as a separate document.

With the Chart Window active on screen:
>> Click on File.
   Click on Save As.
   Place the cursor in the name box and use the delete or backspace key to delete the name suggested.
   Type the name you want to give your file.
   Click on OK.

Once your chart has been saved with a name you can save any changes to the chart by selecting File, Save, OK.

Note: A chart derives its information from the original spreadsheet. You *must* save both the chart *and* the spreadsheet. If you don't save the spreadsheet you will not be able to re-load the chart at a later date because the source information wasn't saved.

Printing a chart

Each chart is printed as a separate document.
>> Click on Chart.
   Click on Select Chart.
   Click on File.
   Click on Page Setup.
   Click on Use Full Page.
   Click on Print.
   Click in the Preview check box.
   Click on OK.

A miniature view of how your printed chart will look will appear on screen. You can look at any part in a magnified view by placing the magnifying glass cursor over the point you want to view and clicking on the mouse. (Click on Zoom to zoom back out).

>> Click on Print.

Your chart will print and should look similar to the chart below.

You have now seen how to create a column chart and use some of the formatting and customising features to adapt it to suit you. The other chart types are customised in a similar way but not all formatting options are available for all types of chart. Try practising with different chart formats and changing them. With practice you should be able to produce charts both quickly and easily.

Answers to Exercise 1

Island Leisure Centre

Opening hours

| Monday to Friday | 10.00 a.m. to 9.00 p.m. |
| Saturdays and Sundays | 10.00 a.m. to 5.30 p.m. |

Facilities

Facilities	Max. no. of persons
Sauna	5
(closed Tuesdays and Thursdays)	
Conditioning room	12
Squash courts	12
Swimming pool	75
Sunbeds	2

Costs (per person/per half hour)

Sauna	£2.50
Conditioning room	£2.00
Squash	£2.50
Swimming pool	£1.80
Sunbed	£2.50

Use of Island Leisure Centre for week beginning 9 September

Day	Facility				
	Sauna	Conditioning	Squash	Swimming Pool	Sunbed
Monday	7	105	30	600	6
Tuesday	X	150	45	800	10
Wednesday	10	150	60	700	8
Thursday	X	180	78	600	15
Friday	23	125	57	1300	12
Saturday	32	110	75	1100	24
Sunday	28	75	30	1100	20
Total	100	895	375	6200	95
Revenue	£250.00	£1,790.00	£937.50	£11,160.00	£237.50

Total revenue   £14,375.00

	Facility				
	Sauna	Conditioning	Squash	Swimming Pool	Sunbed
Average daily use	14	128	54	886	14
Max. no.	32	180	78	1300	24
Min. no.	0	75	30	600	6

Average no. of people using centre each day

Monday	150
Tuesday	201
Wednesday	186
Thursday	175
Friday	303
Saturday	268
Sunday	251